AF426965

A Year to a Better You
The Daily Devotional

Table of Contents

FREEDOM

IDENTITY

LOVE

Introduction

Welcome to *A Year to a Better You*! By joining us in this year long journey, you have committed to learn more about God's Word, about God, and about yourself. It will be a journey of self-discovery and one that, over the course of the coming year, will result in a better you!

In *A Year to a Better You – The Daily Devotional*, we will start in Week 1 with an overview (or review for those who've used it before) of the S.O.A.P. Bible Study Method as we begin our transformation. In Week 2, we'll discover through God's Word the goal of this study and how it can help us in our daily lives as believers. As Week 3 begins, we will dive into our study of God's Word in earnest as we learn all about transparency as believers, freedom in Christ, our identity in Him, and the power of His faithful love.

In *A Year to a Better You – SOAP Journal*, we will do daily readings and use the SOAP Bible Study Method to take our study deeper each day as we read through the entire Bible in a year!

Are you ready? Let's get started!

SOAP

Week One: Transformation
Day 1 - Set the Stage

Whether you are a new believer or a seasoned one, expanding your knowledge of God's Word is done best by spending time there daily. Filled to the brim with God's promises, the Bible also overflows with messages of hope, love, wisdom, and knowledge. Even better, as you study God's Word, you grow in your relationship with Him. There are many ways to study God's Word, but during our year together, we will be using the S.O.A.P. Devotional method to study, grow our faith, and deepen our relationship with God.

S.O.A.P. is an acronym. Do you know what it stands for?

____

S.O.A.P. represents Scripture, Observation, Application, and Prayer, and it only requires a Bible, a time, a place, and in this instance, a copy of this study. As we study the Word together, we'll also do daily personal readings using the S.O.A.P. devotional method.

1. Scripture – Write out the verse which catches your attention.

2. Observation – Note the context of the passage or verse.

3. Application – Consider what God is saying to you.

4. Prayer – Pray God's Word back to Him, affirming His truths.

Day 2 – Focus

The objective of *A Year to a Better You* is to slow you down, to spend time with God in His Word, and to meditate on it. You'll likely be amazed at how much the Holy Spirit will reveal to your heart and mind when you do!

Taking your time with each passage opens the door wide for God to speak with you. No real transformation can take place without the Word of God having a primary role in your life.

Open your Bible and read Joshua 1. For many of us, this is a familiar passage. Write a brief summary of what is happening here.

____

____

____

____

You can chose how you summarize what is happening. Keep in mind our objective is to learn more about God and how we can grow in our relationship with Him. A great way to do so is to look for what God is doing in each and every passage.

As we close today write out the verse from this passage which stands out to you.

____

____

____

____

Day 3 – Foundation

Let's reread Joshua 1 today, taking a closer look at the context of the passage, and asking God to open your heart to what He wants you to notice. As you read, use these questions to help you discover more about the context.

1. What is taking place in the verse(s)?

____

2. To whom is it happening? Why is it happening?

____

3. Who is the audience (who is the passage addressing?)

____

4. Are there any words or phrases repeated?

____

5. Do you see a lesson or theme?

____

Joshua 1 is a pivotal time in the lives of the Israelites who have been delivered from slavery at the hands of the Egyptians and because of their sin have wandered in the wilderness for forty years. Here God commissions Joshua to lead them into the Promised Land after Moses' death. Joshua 1 is filled with encouragement and reassurance but also instruction and inspiration. It is a prompt call to courage and faith during transition. The people must move forward and continually put their faith in their faithful and loving God in order to achieve the BEST He has for them. The same is true for us as Christ followers.

Day 4 – Reflect

As we reflect on Joshua 1, we take a closer look at how to apply God's Word and make it truly personal. To help us gain a greater understanding of what God is saying to us directly, let's ask these questions:

1.   What is God saying to me?

____

2.   How can I apply this to my life? (instruction, encouragement, comfort, guidance)

____

3.   What changes do I need to make, if any, based on what God is telling me personally?

____

The application, no matter how broad it seems (it applies to all believers), also applies uniquely to you because God's Word is always personal, distinct to you.

In Joshua 1:7-8, we read, "Be strong and very courageous. Be careful to obey all the instructions Moses gave you. Do not deviate from them, turning either to the right or to the left. Then you will be successful in everything you do. Study this Book of Instruction continually. Meditate on it day and night so you will be sure to obey everything written in it. Only then will you prosper and succeed in all you do." One application we can easily see that is applicable to all of us as we seek "a year to a better you" is the command to study God's Word, meditate on it, and obey it. Let's pray as we close for the courage and faith to do just that!

Day 5 – Journal: Affirmations

Today is the day we journal our thoughts, pen a prayer, or write affirmations
we have discovered as a result of our study this week. You don't need any
special words. There is no right or wrong. If you are journaling your thoughts, be
completely honest and transparent. If you are praying, talk to God in the same way
you would talk to your best friend. Here's an affirmation to get you started.

If I obey God's instructions, I will be successful in all I do.

Week 2: Getting into the Word with God
Day 1 – Set the Stage

We learned last week the importance of being strong and courageous, putting our faith in God, so that we can live life successfully. We saw God encourage Joshua to read and study His Word day and night, and to obey it so he would be prosperous and successful. God also promised to be with Joshua wherever he went and to never fail or abandon him. The chapter is filled with encouragement and reassurance, instruction and inspiration, all of which we can apply to our own lives. The instructions given to Joshua are guidelines for us to live a strong and courageous, prosperous and successful life as believers.

Today, we head back to the Old Testament and focus our attention on Deuteronomy 17:14-20 where we will find the basis for our year-long journey to better selves. Read this passage and consider how it fits with what we read in Joshua 1. Write your thoughts here.

____

____

____

____

____

This passage offers a bit of foreshadowing. It is from the time Moses is still leading the people. In fact, it is part of the Book of the Law which Joshua was charged with reading and meditating on day and night.

Day 2 – Focus

Today, we'll focus as we reread Deuteronomy 17:14-20 together.

Write a brief summary of what is happening here.

____

____

____

____

____

Keep in mind our objective is to learn more about God and how we can grow in our relationship with Him.

Why do you think God is telling the Israelites rules for rulers and kings, when the nation has none?

____

____

God knew the Israelites would one day ask for a king like the other countries around them had, even though He desired to set them apart by being their King. Here He sets out instructions for the future kings to follow and prosper.

As we close today write out the verse from this passage which stands out to you.

____

____

Day 3 – Foundation

Let's dive into the context of the passage, asking God to open your heart to what He wants to teach you. As you read, use these questions to help you discover more about the context.

1. What is taking place in the verse(s)?

____

2. To whom is it happening? Why is it happening?

____

3. Who is the audience (who is the passage addressing?)

____

4. Are there any words or phrases repeated?

____

5. Do you see a lesson or theme?

____

Long before the Kingdom period began, God gave instructions to what future kings should do each day. God commanded that the king should read the law, write out his own copy of what he read, keep it by his side continually, and reread it daily. If the king obeyed, he and his descendants would reign successfully over the kingdom of Israel for many years.

Day 4 – Reflect

As we take our time reflecting on this passage from the Book of the Law, let's take a closer look to see how we can make it personal and apply it to our lives. To help us gain a greater understanding of what God is saying to us, let's ask these questions:

1. What is God saying to me?

____

2.   How can I apply this to my life? (instruction, encouragement, comfort, guidance)

____

3.   What changes do I need to make, if any, based on what God is telling me personally?

____

Like the kings of Israel who were to come, we learn in this passage what is needed for success whether by consequences or by wisdom. The consequences often cost more than we have to spend, and only become evident after we make a mistake. Wisdom, on the other hand, teaches the needed lesson before the mistake, saving us the pain and heartache of the consequences.

We gain knowledge, understanding, and insight in similar fashion, reading, writing, and repeating, and that is the reason for this study. The king was commanded to read the Word, write it, keep it by his side, and read it daily. We should do the same and therein lies the foundation for this year long journey to our better selves. May we be encouraged, inspired, and challenged along the way!

Day 5 – Journal: Affirmations

Let's journal our thoughts, write a prayer, or note the affirmations we have discovered as a result of our study this week. Remember there is no right or wrong, no specific words you need to use. Here's an affirmation from our reading to get you started.

By reading, writing, and studying God's Word, I can learn to have a deep respect, reverence, and awe for the Lord.

TRANSPARENCY

Week 3: Come Out of Hiding – Take Off the False Self

Day 1 – Set the Stage

As we begin our journey to better selves in earnest, today we'll set the stage to come out of hiding. Let's begin with a question, "Which is more important - knowing God or knowing yourself?"

____

While the 21st Century church often emphasizes knowing God, we also need to know ourselves. The early church fathers understood the significance of both and eagerly taught the connection between knowing God and knowing ourselves. John Calvin proclaimed, "Nearly the whole of sacred doctrine consist in these two parts: knowledge of God and ourselves." Augustine regularly prayed, "Grant, Lord, that I may know myself, that I may know thee." These are just two of many examples of what the early church fathers knew to be true - we must know God and know ourselves.

Focusing on God while failing to know ourselves produces a veneer of piety, leaving a gap between appearance and reality. We look the part on the outside, but transformation and breakthrough can't take place because head knowledge of God and little knowledge of self can't lead to real change. Why is this?

____

We must know ourselves deeply to know God deeply and we must know God deeply to truly know ourselves. If you don't know you are in need, you will never know God as a provider. If you don't know you are broken, you will never know God as a healer. If you don't know you are lost in sin, you will never know God as Savior...

Day 2 - Focus

Read Genesis 2:25-3:11. What or who causes the change in Adam and Eve's perspective? How?

____

____

We got to the place of dissonance and disconnectedness about who we truly are because (from the very beginning) one of the consequences of sin is to give us an identity different from the one God created us to have. It is exactly what happened to Adam and Eve. God created them in His image with a unique identity, sin distorted that identity, and they tried to hide their true identity.

God created us, as humans, in uniqueness. Sin marred that uniqueness. One of the big reasons God sent His Son (the Second Adam) is to restore us to our original uniqueness and true identity in Christ. It is also why knowing ourselves and dealing with ourselves allows us to discover and live our true selves to fulfill our God-given purpose – which is the path to happiness, peace, and our best life!

Is sin in your life distorting your true uniqueness and identity in Christ?

____

____

Tomorrow we'll learn how to apply this truth, confess our sin, get to know ourselves better, and stop hiding our true identity in Christ. It begins with getting to know ourselves better, ceasing to hide our true identity, and taking off our false self.

Day 3 – Foundation

Jesus came to restore us to our true selves, to the unique identity God created us to have, but in order to do so, He needs our cooperation and willingness to acknowledge and take off our false selves. In our Genesis passage, we see Satan lie to Adam and Eve about their identity. They were, after all, already like God, created in His image. Not only did they believe they needed to be like God but the core of the lie they believed was they could be like God apart from God. It's impossible!

When we choose to live a life separate from God, we are living the life of the false self. Think of a time when you tried to live apart from God, do your own thing, or live in your own power – what was the result?

____

____

____

____

____

When we attempt to live apart from God, outside His will for our lives, we are seeking to gain more than the best of everything God offers and the result is we usually end up with less than nothing. When we are living a life of lies and illusions, our money, possessions, status, and accomplishments bolster our false self. Ultimately we lose our authenticity, our true identity. In doing so, we also damage our relationship with Christ, which is exactly what the enemy wants us to do.

Day 4 - Reflect

What characterizes us when we are living in our false selves? These are the common symptoms of a false self:

- Defensiveness – Our false selves need to be kept intact and defensiveness allows us maintain our false identity when we feel attacked.

- Pettiness – Our false selves are based on small "things" of little value, making our false selves small-minded and overly concerned about these "things."

- Pet Peeves – Our false selves focus on what bothers us about others – our pet-peeves. In Matthew 7:3, Jesus explains, the speck that bothers us in someone else is almost always the log in our own eye!

Can you identify these characteristics in your life? Which one or more do you need to take off?

____

____

Read Proverbs 21:2. What truth is found here?

____

____

The Lord looks inside, directly at our hearts, seeing that which even we can't discern when we are living in our false selves.

Ask God to help you take off your false self ("being right in your own eyes") so you can measure up when "the Lord examines your heart."

Day 5 – Journal - Affirmations

Today, let's journal affirmations, thoughts, and prayers, based on what we have learned. Remember, there are no right or wrong ways to journal – write down what God has taught you, what He wants you to do today, or a simple prayer (thanks, guidance, praise, or requests). Here's an affirmation to get you started.

I am made in the image of God, I don't need to put on a false self.

Week 4: Come Out of Hiding – Follow Jesus in Rejecting a False Self

Day 1 – Set the Stage

Last week, as we worked toward transparency, we came to understand the importance of knowing ourselves and knowing God. We realized because we are created in the image of God, we don't need to put on a false self. This week we are going to learn how we can follow Jesus and reject a false self.

During His time on earth, Jesus remained fully God but He was also fully human. As a human being, like us, He had to find Himself and in doing so He must have been tempted by many false ways of living His life. In fact, we know He was because we have a record of some of His temptations. Let's read Matthew 4:1-11 together.

> Then Jesus was led by the Spirit into the wilderness to be tempted by the devil. After fasting forty days and forty nights, he was hungry. The tempter came to him and said, "If you are the Son of God, tell these stones to become bread." Jesus answered, "It is written: 'Man shall not live on bread alone, but on every word that comes from the mouth of God.'" Then the devil took him to the holy city and had him stand on the highest point of the temple. "If you are the Son of God," he said, "throw yourself down. For it is written: "'He will command his angels concerning you, and they will lift you up in their hands, so that you will not strike your foot against a stone.'" Jesus answered him, "It is also written: 'Do not put the Lord your God to the test.'" Again, the devil took him to a very high mountain and showed him all the kingdoms of the world and their splendor. "All this I will give you," he said, "if you will bow down and worship me." Jesus said to him, "Away from me, Satan! For it is written: 'Worship the Lord your God, and serve him only.'" Then the devil left him, and angels came and attended him.

What three major potential false self-temptations is Jesus faced with?

____

____

____

Day 2 – Focus

Let's reread Matthew 4:1-11 as we begin. Yesterday, we asked what three major potential false self-temptations Jesus faced. Today, let's focus on and unpack them.

After forty days of fasting, Jesus would have been ravenous. It is not surprising the enemy attacked through His hunger, His appetite. Jesus's hunger was real and genuine, but the way Satan tempted Him to fulfill His hunger was illegitimate. The same is true in our lives. How has Satan tried to tempt you to fulfill a legitimate hunger (appetite) in an illegitimate way?

____

____

____

The enemy's first attempt at tempting Jesus to put on a false self was by suggesting He turn stones into bread. It was a temptation to power – the very same thing the enemy does to us!

How did Jesus reject the enemy's temptation to a false self?

____

____

____

Jesus said no to the invitation to establish His identity on the basis of His actions, particularly when it came to doing something independent of His submission to the authority of God.

Day 3 – Foundation

In Matthew 4, Satan's first temptation of Jesus was to power. Next, the devil invited Jesus to throw Himself from the top of the temple into the crowd below, so they would immediately recognize Him as the Messiah. It was a temptation to prestige. And yes, the enemy loves to use this one on us as well. How has the enemy tempted you to prestige (status, reputation, fame)?

____

____

How did Jesus reject the temptation?

____

____

Jesus rejected the temptation, choosing not to base his identity on prestige but rather on His identity in the Father, not what people thought of Him.

In the final temptation to put on a false self, Satan offered Jesus all the kingdoms of the world. It was a temptation of possessions. It is a temptation we all face, often on a daily basis as we are bombarded at every turn with advertisements and influences. How did Jesus reject this temptation to a false self?

____

____

Jesus rejected the offer to put on a false self once more, refusing to find His identity in possessions. He knew Himself in terms of poverty of spirit and the loving will of the Father.

Day 4 – Reflect

As we reflect on our study this week, reread Matthew 4:1-11. Jesus rejected Satan's temptations to put on a false self. He knew power was a poor substitute for His relationship with the Father. Jesus knew who He was in God and that knowledge was the foundation for His ability to resist temptations to put on a false self and live from a false center based on power, prestige, or possessions. By resisting these false ways of being, Jesus moved toward an identity grounded in His relationship to the Father—an identity in which His calling became obvious as He came to understand who He really was.

Jesus understood that building our identity apart from God does not lead to freedom but to bondage. What false self do you need to follow Jesus in rejecting? How can you use Jesus example to do so?

____

____

____

Every moment of every day of our lives, God seeks our companionship. Often He can't find us because we are hiding in our false selves. He continues to pursue us, calling us into a relationship with Himself. The more we identify with our psychologically constructed selves, our financially constructed selves...the more deeply we hide from God, as well as ourselves and others. Coming out of hiding requires us embrace the vulnerabilities that first sent us scurrying for cover and follow Jesus in rejecting our false selves. As long as we try to pretend things are not as they are, we choose falsity. Instead we need to come out of hiding and take a step toward honesty with our selves.

Day 5 – Journal - Affirmations

Today, as we journal our affirmations, thoughts, and prayers, based on what we have learned, remember there is no right or wrong way. Write down what God has taught you, what He wants you to do in light of His teaching, or compose a simple prayer of thanks, guidance, praise, or requests). Here's an affirmation to get you started.

Like me, Jesus was tempted to put on a false self while on earth, but like Jesus I can reject the enemy's temptation and instead embrace who I am in the Father.

Week 5: Knowing Yourself - Knowing Yourself As Deeply Loved

Day 1 - Set the Stage

As we continue our journey to transparency, putting off our false selves, and knowing our true selves, let's read Ephesians 3:17b-19.

> "... And I pray that you, being rooted and established in love, may have power, together with all the Lord's holy people, to grasp how wide and long and high and deep is the love of Christ, and to know this love that surpasses knowledge—that you may be filled to the measure of all the fullness of God."

What do you learn after reading this short passage?

____

____

____

In order for us to fully be ourselves, we must know ourselves and doing so begins by knowing ourselves as we are known by God. It is exactly what Paul is communicating in this passage to the believers in Ephesus.

Genuine self-knowledge begins by looking at God and seeing how God is looking at us. Grounding our knowledge of ourselves in God's knowledge of ourselves anchors us in His truth. It also anchors us in God.

God doesn't simply like us. God doesn't simply have warm affection for us because we are created in His image. God loves each and every one of us with depth, persistence, and intensity beyond imagination.

Day 2 – Focus

Yesterday we learned God loves us with depth, persistence, and intensity beyond imagination. He loves us with what one scholar calls "a passionate absorbed interest." In Isaiah 49:16, God says, "See, I have written your name on the palms of my hands." God cannot help seeing us though eyes of love. Even more incredible, God's love for us as nothing to do with our behavior!

Read John 3:16-17. How does this passage testify to God's great love for us?

____

____

____

____

____

Neither our faithfulness nor our unfaithfulness alters God's love for us in the slightest. If you have time today, read Luke 15:11-32, Jesus's parable of the prodigal son. The familiar parable gives the best illustration of the Father's love – absolutely unconditional, unlimited, and unimaginably extravagant. Paul says it is so high, no matter how high up we go; it is so wide, no matter how far left or right we are; and it is so low, no matter how low we fall (Ephesians 3:17b-19) – God's love is always there!

Love is our identity and our calling, for we are children of love – created from love, of love, and for love, our existence makes no sense apart from God's love. The desire to know God and know ourselves can't progress very far unless it begins with a knowledge of how deeply we are loved by God.

Day 3 - Foundation

A huge part of understanding how deeply loved by God we are comes when we understand nothing can separate us from God's love – nothing we could do or fail to do, nor anything that could be done to us by someone else. Read Romans 8:35-39 and make a list of all the things listed which CANNOT separate us from God's love.

____

____

____

If we don't understand these truths, then we remain in kindergarten when it comes to spiritual development. In order for our knowledge of God's love to be truly transformational, it must be the foundation of our identity, who we experience ourselves to be – the "I" each of us carries within. An identity grounded in God means when we think of who we are, the first thing that comes to mind is our status as an individual deeply loved by God. (Who we are is NOT what we do!)

Read Matthew 3:13-17. From whom or what did Jesus actions flow?

____

____

Everything Jesus did flowed out of his understanding of how much God loved Him. Even when Jesus felt God had abandoned Him in the Garden of Gethsemane, His confidence in the love of the Father was so great He still desired God's will over His own. Jesus knew He was deeply loved by the Father whether or not He felt it. His identity was grounded in God.

Day 4 - Reflect

The Bible is full of examples of how knowing the depth of God's love for us is able to transform us. Read John 4:1-26. What is the significance of the Samaritan woman's meeting and conversation with Jesus at the well?

Samaritans were considered outcasts by the Jews. As such, the Samaritan woman was astounded by the way Jesus treated her. He approached her rather than avoiding her. He engaged her in conversation. Even later when He exposed her moral failings, He did not condemn her. He revealed her to herself. He revealed Himself to her as the Messiah. She was touched by His perfect love and would never be the same!

Read John 4:27-42 for the rest of the story. What was the result of her transformation by God's love?

Every time we dare to meet God in the vulnerability of our sin and shame, we open the door to experience the depth of His love. We only know God's unconditional, radical, and reckless love for us when we approach Him just as we are. The more we have the courage to meet God in our weakness, the more we know how truly and deeply we are loved by God.

Day 5 – Journal: Affirmations

We've learned a lot this week. Today, let's take a few minutes to journal our affirmations, thoughts, and prayers, based on what we have learned. Write down what God has taught you, what He wants you to do in light of His teaching, or compose a simple prayer of thanks, guidance, praise, or requests. Here's an affirmation to get you started.

God's love for me is unconditional, unlimited, and unimaginably extravagant.

Week 6: Knowing Yourself - Knowing Your Ignored Parts of Self

Day 1 - Set the Stage

Last week, we learned how knowing we are truly and deeply loved by God helps us know ourselves better - through God's eyes of love. This week, we'll uncover how to encounter and embrace the unwelcomed parts of ourselves, our previously ignored parts of self. We all tend to think of ourselves as a single, unified self, but what we call "I" is really a "family" of many part selves. While that is not a particular problem, the real problem lies in the fact that many of the part selves are unknown to us. We often remain blissfully oblivious to their existence, thought they are usually known to others.

In truth, there are important aspects about ourselves that we continually ignore. For instance, we refuse to face our feelings of shame because they make us feel too vulnerable. We pretend they do not exist, hoping they will disappear. It may be our broken, wounded self we deny, but even so, they don't go away, only into hiding. If, for example, we only know our strong, competent selves, we are never able to embrace our weak or insecure selves and so we are forced to live a lie, pretending we are strong and competent. If we refuse to face our deceitful selves, we live an illusion regarding our own integrity. If we are unwilling to acknowledge our prideful selves, we live an illusion of our humility.

There is enormous value in naming and coming knowing these excluded parts of self. List yours here and acknowledge their presence.

____

____

____

Day 2 - Focus

Yesterday we acknowledged our ignored parts of self. Powerful conditioning in our childhoods encouraged us to acknowledge only the most acceptable parts of our selves. These excluded parts are not given a place at the family table but even so they become stronger, not weaker. Operating out of sight and beyond awareness, they have increasing influence on who we are. It is part of the reason we do things in the dark because parts of ourselves live there. A crucial portion of spiritual growth involves acknowledging all our part selves, exposing them to God's love, and letting Him weave them into the new person He is crafting.

Read Ephesians 5:11. What is the warning here?

____

____

We must be willing to welcome these ignored parts as full members of the family of self, giving them space at the family table, slowly allowing them to be healed by love and integrated into the whole person we are becoming. Allowing God to accept us just as we are helps us to accept ourselves the same way. It is essential for genuine spiritual transformation.

Self-acceptance and self-knowing are deeply interconnected. To truly know ourselves, we must accept all our parts – those areas we most deeply want to change must first be accepted – even embraced. Self-transformation is always preceded by self-acceptance. The self we must accept is the self we actually and truly are and it has to be done before we start our self-improvement projects!

Day 3 - Foundation

Any hope for knowing ourselves without accepting the excluded parts of self we wish weren't true is an illusion. Reality must be embraced before it can be changed. Knowing ourselves will remain superficial until we are willing to accept ourselves as God accepts us - fully and unconditionally, just as we are. God's acceptance of us, as well as our acceptance of ourselves, just as we are does not in any way conflict with God's intent for us to be transformed. Yet, until we are prepared to accept the selves we truly are, we block God's transforming work of making us into our true selves in Christ. We must befriend the self we seek to know. We must receive it with hospitality, not hostility. No one can be known apart from such a welcome. Read Luke 5:4-10. How does Peter set the example for us in this?

____

____

Peter acknowledges he is a sinner and Jesus still says follow Me. If God loves and accepts us as sinners, how can we do any less?

Read Matthew 26:31-35. What does Jesus understand about Peter even after their early encounter? (This event is also recorded in Luke 22:31-34 and John 21:15-19.)

____

____

Even though Jesus had accepted Peter, He still knew there was some stuff Peter hadn't acknowledged. You can never be other than who you are until you are willing to embrace the reality of who you are. Only then can you truly become who you are most deeply called to be.

Day 4 – Reflect

As we reflect, we need to understand crucifixion should be directed toward our sin nature. We must first accept it as our nature, not simply human nature. Only after we genuinely know and accept everything, can we find within ourselves the ability to begin to develop the discernment to know what should be crucified and what should be embraced. The things which we refuse to acknowledge are given increased power and influence by our failure to accept them. It's what we avoid which causes the most problems in our lives.

Self-acceptance does not increase the power of things which ultimately need to be eliminated, rather, it weakens them because it robs them of the power they develop when they operate outside of awareness and self-acceptance. Often when we seek what is missing in our lives, we look where we can easily search rather than in the dark where it hides.

Read Matthew 6:6. Where can we go to encounter God and transform our lives?

____

____

The secret place we encounter God in a truly transformational way is in our inner selves. Prayer is meeting God in the secret place. God wants complete access to the dark parts of our soul that most need transformation. What dark parts do you need to acknowledge and accept so God can transform you?

____

____

Day 5 – Journal - Affirmations

As we close our week, let's take a few minutes to journal our affirmations, thoughts, and prayers, based on what we have learned. You can include what God has taught you, what He wants you to do in light of His teaching, or compose a simple prayer of thanks, guidance, praise, or requests. Here's an affirmation to get you started.

God wants complete access to the dark parts of my soul that most need transformation because He love me deeply.

Week 7: Knowing Yourself as You Really Are – Knowing Yourself as a Sinner

Day 1 – Set the Stage

As we continue our quest toward transparency and understanding of ourselves as we truly are, let's consider what we've discovered thus far. Knowing the depths of God's personal love for each of us as individuals is the foundation of all genuine self-knowledge. The self that God persistently loves is not our prettied-up pretend selves but our actual selves – the real us!

Take a moment as we begin this week to compare and/or contrast.

Your Real Self	Your Ideal Self
_____________________	_____________________
_____________________	_____________________
_____________________	_____________________

The problem is, we are all masters of delusion. Often, we have trouble penetrating our own web of self-deceptions and knowing our true selves. We continually confuse our genuine selves with some ideal self we wish we were. For many of us, the roots of our pretend selves lie in our childhood which taught us we could secure love by presenting ourselves in the most flattering light. In short, we learned to fake it. While it is innocent as children, the problem is as we grow older, we lose touch with reality. Theologian Thomas Merton describe it this way, "There is no greater disaster in spiritual life than to be immersed in unreality, for life is maintained and nourished in us by our vital relation with reality." We can all relate.

The truth is most of us are quite willing to embrace reality when it fits how we see ourselves and the world and is not overly unpleasant. However, when life confronts us with things about ourselves we are unwilling to accept, we call on psychological defense mechanisms to help us maintain a sense of safety and stability. While these unconscious strategies help with short-term coping, they block long-term growth because they distort reality.

Read Jeremiah 17:9. What point is God making about self-deception?

____

____

Our hearts are deceitful with a great capacity for self-deception. The issue is self-deception often happens automatically. It is a portion of what psychologists mean when they explain how our defense mechanisms often operate in our unconscious. These defense mechanisms come in various forms but some of the most common are:

- Reaction Formation – Some unacceptable feeling or impulse is eliminated from our awareness by our expression of its opposite.

- Rationalization – We give a reason for our behavior, but not the real reason.

- Denial – We deny or ignore feelings that are obviously present.

Which have you used before? Why?

____

____

How can knowing this help you find the truth?

____

Day 3 – Foundation

Having identified our propensity for deceitfulness and our use of defense mechanisms this week, today we'll discover another important way to understand them. These defense mechanisms are exactly what original sin is all about.

Read Luke 15:1-2. How did Jesus respond to sinners? Why do you think this shocked the religious leaders of the day?

____

____

____

Jesus welcomed sinners, which is good for us, since we are all sinners. Knowing ourselves as we really are (sinners) and facing our tendencies for self-deception brings us face to face with what the Bible calls "sin" and what theologians call the "original sin." It doesn't take a lot of self-awareness to recognize the very basic things about us that are not as they should be.

Take a moment to note areas in your life which may not be as they should be or as you want them to be.

____

____

____

We are not alone in this, in fact, Paul bemoans it in Romans 7 saying, "I do not understand what I do. For what I want to do I do not do, but what I hate I do." Don't get discouraged, knowing yourself as a sinner is part of the journey to a better you!

Day 4 – Reflect

Read Romans 7:15-23. What is Paul saying? How does it relate to us as sinners?

____

____

____

____

____

If we are honest about our day-to-day lives, our testimony is exactly like Paul's. Author James Finley describes it like this.

> There is something in me that puts on fig leaves of concealment, kills my brother, builds towers of confusion, and brings cosmic chaos upon the earth. There is something in me that loves darkness rather than light, that rejects God and thereby rejects my own deepest reality as a human person made in the image and likeness of God.

Some Christians base their identity on being a sinner, which is not completely accurate. The truth is we are deeply loved sinners. We were created in the good, sinless image of God, for love and by love. And although sin damaged that image and identity, it allowed us to discover God's unconditional love for us because He loves us just as we are, as sinners. Look back at Luke 15:1-2. How did Jesus respond to sinners?

____

A true understanding of sin is not based on morality, it is based on knowing ourselves.

Day 5 – Journal: Affirmations

Looking at sin and recognizing ourselves as sinners is not an easy task, but we did it! As we journal this week, confess your sin and self-deception as God continues to shower you with his great love and welcome you and fellowship with you. Journal your affirmations, thoughts, and prayers, based on what you have learned. Here's an affirmation to get you started.

Although sin damaged my image and identity created in His image, it allowed me to discover God's unconditional love for me because He loves me just as I am — a sinner saved by grace.

Week 8: Knowing Yourself as You Really Are – Getting Behind Sins to Sin
Day 1 – Set the Stage

Let's read Psalm 51:5 as we begin this week. What does David remind us?

____

____

David tells us to be human is to be a sinner, to be broken, and to wear an image different from the good, sinless image and identity God created and intended for us. Knowing this is crucial in our quest to know ourselves as we truly are. In order to do so, we must acknowledge and recognize our natural human tendencies to be fleshly and sinful, to try to hide our true selves behind fig leaves as Adam and Eve did. Real spiritual transformation does not result from trying to fix our own problems and sinfulness, but results from turning to God in the midst of them and meeting God just as we are. Turning to God in our sin and shame and fig-leaf-covering-up-selves is the heart of spiritual transformation.

What sin or shame do you need to turn from?

____

____

Write a short prayer asking God to help you turn to Him and meet Him in the midst of it this week and let the spiritual transformation begin.

____

____

Day 2 – Focus

Today, let's read Luke 6:6-10 together.

> On another Sabbath he went into the synagogue and was teaching, and a man was there whose right hand was shriveled. The Pharisees and the teachers of the law were looking for a reason to accuse Jesus, so they watched him closely to see if he would heal on the Sabbath. But Jesus knew what they were thinking and said to the man with the shriveled hand, "Get up and stand in front of everyone." So he got up and stood there. Then Jesus said to them, "I ask you, which is lawful on the Sabbath: to do good or to do evil, to save life or to destroy it?" He looked around at them all, and then said to the man, "Stretch out your hand." He did so, and his hand was completely restored.

From this passage, what do you learn about sin and God's ability to heal?

____

____

____

____

The bottom line here is that God cannot heal what we continue to conceal. When the man stretched out his hand, he was completely restored. It is what we all want, isn't it – to get to the bottom of our sin and allow God to transform us.

The question is how do we get behind the sins causing us to sin? There is something behind the fig leaves, there is something behind the way we cover up, there is even something behind the sins we commit. In order to know ourselves as we really are we have to get behind the stuff we do to the core of why we do it! Essentially everything we do is a major sin area or an area of brokenness we are trying to hide and until we see it for what it is we will be controlled by it and live in bondage to it! God cannot heal what you conceal!

Day 3 – Foundation

Most of us realize how simple it is to sin, but do we also understand all the factors which contribute to sin? The problem is sin can appear complex but in reality it is simple. Let's discover just how simple it is.

Read 1 John 5:17. What is sin?

____

____

Read James 1:14-15. Why do we sin? What is the final result of sin?

____

____

Sin is all wrongdoing. Why we sin isn't all that complicated either, our sin comes from our desires. Sin at its most foundational level manifest itself from the fact that we believe disobeying God will make us happier than obeying God. It doesn't matter if we actively commit the sin or just dwell on it in the dark places of our hearts and minds (Matthew 5:28). When we sin, we are acting just as Adam and Eve did eating the forbidden fruit in the Garden of Eden (Genesis 3:6). We are essentially replicating the original sin, believing Satan's oft repeated spin on sin – that sinning will make us happier than obeying God.

Read Romans 14:23. How can we apply this truth to our lives to help us break free from believing Satan's lies will make us happier than God's will?

____

____

Day 4 – Reflect

As humans, we are often prisoners of our beliefs, seeking happiness in the wrong places. Jesus explains the premise in John 8:34, when He says, "I tell you the truth, everyone who sins is a slave of sin." Even when we realize the destructive powers of sin and long to be free we often remain captive to sin's power. Why? We believe obedience to God requires self-denial and misery, and so we choose sin believing therein lies happiness.

Read Matthew 16:24-26. What is Jesus's admonition to His followers?

____

____

Breaking free from sin does require a measure of self-denial, but the true defeat of sin occurs when we are driven by a desire for the greatest joy, that which only God can provide. How is it accomplished, this breaking free from sins, getting behind the sins which cause us to sin?

We have to ask ourselves whose promises really deliver true happiness and joy.

____

____

We know the answer – God's promises are better. God's promises are true (2 Corinthians 1:20). The more certain we are of God as the source of all joy, the better equipped we are to know ourselves and the more prepared we are to fight against the temptation and draw of sin.

Day 5 – Journal: Affirmations

As we close out this week, it's time to journal our affirmations, thoughts, and prayers, based on what we have learned. This week, consider asking God to confirm His promises are true and to help you believe He is the source of all joy and happiness. Here's an affirmation to get you started.

God's promises are true and are the source of life's greatest joy and happiness so I can trust Him and resist the enemy's temptation to sin.

Week 9: The Danger of Not Knowing Yourself – You Don't Value & Appreciate The Right Places and The Right People

Day 1 – Set the Stage

We are moving closer and closer to transparency, to knowing ourselves and God better. In doing so, we've learned to take off our false selves and be our authentic selves and we've come to understand that while we are sinners we are also deeply loved by God. Today, we will start examining the danger of not knowing ourselves.

Read Judges 11:1-11. Write a short summary of what is happening here.

____

____

____

____

____

Here we meet Jephthah, son of a distinguished man named Gilead and a prostitute. In a moment of weakness and questionable judgment, his father, Gilead had visited a prostitute which resulted in Jephthah's birth.

In contrast, his brothers were all true sons of Gilead and his wife. They did not carry the stigma of being conceived outside the covenant of marriage, and they had no use for Jephthah, who bore the invisible label "Illegitimate." His brothers drove Jephthah away saying, "You are not going to get any inheritance in our family . . . because you are the son of another woman." No doubt Jephthah had trouble knowing himself and where he fit in to his father's family as well as what his value truly was.

Day 2 – Focus

For his family, Jephthah was a disturbing reminder of Gilead's infidelity as well as the pain and shame his actions caused his family. Every time anyone in the family looked at Jephthah, they remembered, consciously or unconsciously, the embarrassing reason for his existence. Jephthah's mother, as a prostitute, was likely from a non-Hebrew race since Mosaic Law strictly prohibited prostitution, which meant Jephthah's ethnicity was mixed while his brothers were "pure" Israelites. Much like prejudice today, biases and unfair judgments were also common in Jephthah's time and no doubt he endured whispers, condescending looks, and unsavory comments from his community as well as his bothers. His family obviously assumed he would inherit the weaknesses and not the strengths of his father. The problem is all these judgments, feelings, and opinions were not based on anything Jephthah did – it was not his fault!

With this in mind, reread Judges 11:1a. How does God see Jephthah?

____

____

God sees Jephthah as a might warrior. Here the word "mighty" means "courage, valor, substance." It is the way God saw him. Remember we learned knowing yourself and loving yourself begins when we recognize how God sees us. The problem was (and often is for us) Jephthah didn't see himself that way – his sense of self was based on the validation of those around him and his past over which he had no control. We cannot place the truth of who we are in the hands of others who draw conclusions from opinions which are not based in fact. We also shouldn't try to prove those people wrong, especially when we did nothing to form their opinions.

Day 3 – Foundation

In this passage God is teaching us a valuable lesson. We need to value and appreciate the right places and the right people, not those who formed opinions about us not grounded in facts.

Read Judges 11:3 again. Where had Jephthah gone and why? Who was with him?

____

____

Jephthah had settled in Tob (meaning "good"), a haven for exiles, murderers, mercenaries, and thieves, after his brothers drove him away. It was a place on which people cast aspersions as it was a land of criminals and outcasts. Even so, for Jephthah, it was a place of crucial development in his life, according to God's plan and purpose. There, Jephthah got married and began to raise his own family. He developed relationships with a band of adventurers who looked up to him as their leader. They became his band of brothers, poised and positioned to give him the camaraderie, support, and love his biological siblings failed to provide. His biological brothers didn't recognize his uniqueness, but God and these people did!

Can you relate to Jephthah? How?

____

____

What makes us special, valuable, and unique is not determined by those who can't see it, but by those who can. At first, Jephthah can't see it himself, but God can...

Day 4 - Reflect

Our inability to receive from those who love and value us often results because we are still defined by people who don't see our value. It indicates we don't truly know who we are. It was true for Jephthah in Tob even though his life there was flourishing. He couldn't see it, value it, or appreciate it because he was so imprisoned by his past. He couldn't see the very things he had always hungered for—the love and acceptance of his family, approval, community, a sense of belonging—had become realities because he kept looking for them in the sources of his past.

Is it true for you where you are today? Explain.

____

____

____

Jephthah's presence in Tob was providential, but he didn't know it. He couldn't let go of the ideal of his family's love. He still had an unhealed wound festering in his heart. Many of us are in a good place, but fail to recognize it because of past pain. It is the big lesson from Jephthah's story. We have to trust God to lead us, we have to value the places He puts us. Sometimes those places and experiences which we deemed bad are blessings in disguise. We have to learn to view ourselves and our circumstances from God's perspective or we will miss the wonderful plans God has for us! Instead, we spend our time longing for the something from our past that isn't His best for us. Sometimes God causes people or places others may regard as lowly to be the ideal environments to strengthen us, heal us, and lead us into our destinies. When we are okay with ourselves, we can love the people and the places God brings into our lives.

Day 5 – Journal: Affirmations

As we close our week, let's journal our affirmations, thoughts, and prayers, based on what we have learned. Include what God has taught you, what He wants you to do in light of His teaching, or compose a simple prayer of thanks, guidance, praise, or requests. Here's an affirmation to get you started.

I have to choose not to continue grasping for the people and places that have repeatedly failed or hurt me in the past and to trust completely that God knows what He is doing and is working for my good.

Week 10: The Danger of Not Knowing Yourself – Allowing the Opinions of the Wrong People to Matter and Sacrificing the Wrong Things

Day 1 – Set the Stage

Last week we learned one of the dangers of not knowing ourselves was not valuing or appreciating the right places and the right people. This week, we'll focus on the danger of allowing the opinions of the wrong people to matter way too much in our lives.

Reread Judges 11:1-11 again. Note anything you see about the opinions of wrong people in regard to Jephthah.

____

____

____

Verses 4-6 say, "Sometime later, when the Ammonites made war on Israel, the elders of Gilead went to get Jephthah from the land of Tob, 'Come,' they said, 'be our commander, so we can fight the Ammonites.'" Jephthah was doing well in Tob, but then his brothers came roaring back into his life, bringing with them all the pain they represented.

They did not come because they realized how much they hurt Jephthah in the past. They did not come to apologize for treating him badly. They did not come because they had matured and recognized they had missed knowing a good and decent person or because they wanted to develop a real relationship with him. They came back because they wanted what Jephthah had and they didn't: courage and military leadership skills.

Day 2 - Focus

The nation of Israel was under attack, and obviously, the brothers had heard about Jephthah's position with his adventurers. Though they had no use or regard for him while they were growing up, now everything dear to them was threatened and they needed his strength, courage, and leadership!

Reread Judges 11:7-11. What do the elders of Gilead promise? Why?

____

____

____

What problems do you see with what transpires in these verses?

____

____

____

Like many of us, Jephthah faced multiple problems. What we accept from people who don't love us says so much about whether or not we love ourselves. When we don't know who we are and when we don't love ourselves, we open ourselves to manipulation. People can smell desperation on us like cheap perfume and desperation leads to manipulation. Self-love and self-awareness commands respect. If we don't love ourselves, we can't expect others to love us.

How often have you, like Jephthah, given those who are underserving a pass?

____

____

Jephthah did not value or appreciate the right places or the right people and instead allowed the opinions of the wrong people to matter most in his life. Can you remember a time in your life when you did the same?

____

____

____

Read Judges 11:29-35. How does Jephthah's story end?

____

____

____

They had promised to give Jephthah a position of leadership in their community. He made the disappointing and detrimental decision to go with them. He left behind the good place God had given him to go back to the place of his pain.

His story unfolds as one of the most heartbreaking accounts in the Bible; the results of his decision are tragic. In his desire to please the wrong people, he made a rash vow to God, promising to offer a burnt offering of sacrifice to Him of whatever came out of his house first when he returned home.

Tragically, when he reached his house, his young daughter came dancing out the door of their home to meet him. To keep his vow to God, he had to sacrifice the girl. He abandoned quality relationships to go with people who had previously rejected him, and his choice cost him dearly.

Read Hebrews 11:32. Jephthah is mentioned here in the familiar passage known as the Hall of Faith. Why?

____

____

Though his story is a challenging one of tragedy, he is remembered in Hebrews because of his faith. We watched as Jephthah suffered because of the sins of others. Jephthah had to deal with the result of his father's sin of unfaithfulness. His brothers rejected him; there was no inheritance. His family turned against him.

Of course God was more concerned about the development of his character. Though he couldn't control his circumstances, he could control his reaction to them. God guided him to Tob where he built not only his strength, but his valor, and also a family. The people there recognized his value and looked to him as a leader.

Though his biological family and his early community rejected him, when life brought challenges their way, they turned to him - the one they had rejected.

People today do the same, forgetting God when things are going well, but calling on Him when times get hard. As believers, we are called to be close to God in all times - good and bad - unconditionally. Jephthah was faithful to God and God was with him every step of the way. Ask God to help you escape the dangers of trusting the wrong people and the wrong things, and to trust Him fully so He can guide you every step of the way.

Day 5 – Journal: Affirmations

Let's take a few minutes to pen a prayer to God asking Him to help us trust Him fully and in all circumstances, to develop our character, and strengthen our faith. Let's journal affirmations from our study this week and note what God wants us to do based on what we've learned.

Here's an affirmation to get you started.

God is with me every step of the way when I trust Him and His plan for my life.

Freedom

Week 11: The Tree of the Knowledge of Good and Evil (TKGE) – Perversion of Truth (Fruits of the TKGE)

Day 1 – Set the Stage

This week we will take our first steps toward true freedom in Christ. Let's begin by reading Genesis 2:16-17. What permission is given? What warning is given?

____

____

____

The Tree of Life is considerably more than a backdrop to the creation story. If we choose, it can be a way of life. In chapter 1 of Genesis, we learn about the creation of the world by God the Creator and Ruler who has authority and dominion over all. In chapter 2, we meet Adam and Eve, are introduced to two trees – The Tree of Life (TOL) and The Tree of the Knowledge of Good and Evil (TKGE), and learn about the original sin. In fact, every story in the Bible hinges on the story in chapter 2. Everyday humanity has to choose everyday between the Tree of Life (a loving, forgiving God, freedom, grace, and eternal life) and the Tree of the Knowledge of Good and Evil (a judgmental God, bondage, the Law, and death).

In Genesis 3, rather than walking in communion with God and freedom, humans were separated from God and in bondage because of sin. Satan perverted the truth about the TKGE, Adam and Eve sinned, and we were separated from God, until God made a way to end the separation and restore our relationship with Him.

Day 2 – Focus

Let's turn our focus to how God made the way to end the separation brought by Satan's perversion of the truth and humankind's sin. Read Colossians 1:19-21. What do you learn about how we can restore our relationship with God.

____

____

It was through Jesus that "God reconciled everything to Himself." Though we were far from God, His enemies in fact, God made a way to restore our relationship with Him. Before we go on, let's turn our focus to God. Every one of us needs to know the starting point to a relationship with God and walking in freedom is accepting you are a sinner and understanding Jesus has paid the penalty for your sin by shedding His blood and dying on a cross. Read Romans 10:9. What is promised?

____

____

The Bible says that if you confess with your mouth and believe with your heart Jesus is Lord and that God raised Him from the dead, you will be saved. If you haven't done so, below is a simple prayer you can use to invite Jesus into your heart as Savior and take your first step toward freedom.

Dear Jesus,

Thank You for dying on the cross and making a way for me to come to God. I receive this extravagant gift and ask You to come into my heart and be the Lord of my life. I give You all of me and ask You to turn my life around for the glory of God. Forgive me of my sin, fill me with Your Spirit, and help me to live the life You died to give me, in Jesus name, Amen.

Day 3 - Foundation

We know the first sin led to separation. Reread Genesis 2:16-17. Now read Genesis 3:1-9. What did Adam and Eve do? What did God do?

____

____

Adam and Eve hid; God came looking for them. God seeks after sinful man because of His great love. He sent His Son, Jesus, to rescue us. Adam and Eve sinned by eating the fruit from the tree forbidden for them – the Tree of the Knowledge of Good and Evil. The fruit of the tree is just that – the knowledge (information, ideas, world view, thoughts) of good and evil. God warned them changing their way of thinking would create separation, making them unable to relate to Him and understand Him. Satan told them otherwise, saying "it won't hurt you to think like that." The issue isn't knowledge, but rather the motive behind the acquisition of knowledge. Were they looking to gain God's wisdom and understanding or were they looking to exalt themselves?

____

Read Colossians 2:2-3. What do we find hidden in Jesus?

____

God also told them the fruit was deadly. Satan didn't tempt Eve with blatant rebellion, but tempted her with the desire to be like God. Often the desire to know is in direct opposition to the desire to trust. We may set out to gain information, ideas, and the data needed to run our lives, in other words, become like God. We can control our lives and be self-sufficient, but in the end we lose our lives.

Day 4 - Reflect

In addition to the fruit of the TKGE as knowledge but also deadly, we also see the fruit is consumed (Genesis 3:6). Eating is not just putting food in your mouth; it is ingesting the food. Ideas are ingested in our minds and then sin is conceived. How did the first sin come about? Eve talked to Adam about it – they had a conversation and worked the idea. They took something outside of themselves and put it inside themselves. Can you think of a personal example to illustrate the danger of consuming certain kinds of knowledge?

____

____

The fruit of the TKGE also causes separation (Genesis 3:8). Remember, Adam and Eve hid from God, He didn't turn His back on them. He looked for them. The truth is Adam and Eve made an incorrect judgment of God – He wasn't waiting for them to fail so He could judge them. God is love and when we see His heart for us, we will run to Him instead of hiding when we sin.

The fruit was deadly because it was satisfying. Knowledge—even without love, wisdom, or understanding—can be satisfying. If we figure out a system of right and wrong and do right, we can be satisfied doing the right things. The problem – God says we can only come to Him through grace, by faith, not works. We can't connect with God by simply doing more good than bad. TKGE thinking leads us to live by a set of rules to make us look good on the outside but the fruit is deadly because we are consumed by what others think of us rather than what God thinks. We need to seek instead wisdom from above (James 3:17). What wisdom are you seeking?

Day 5 - Journal - Affirmations

As we close our week, let's journal our affirmations, thoughts, and prayers, based on what we have learned this week. You can include what God has taught you, what He wants you to do in light of His teaching, or compose a simple prayer of thanks, guidance, praise, or requests. Here's an affirmation to get you started.

God is love. When I recognize His heart for me, I can run to Him instead of hiding my sin.

Week 12: The Tree of the Knowledge of Good and Evil – Deadly Fruits – Shame and Victimization

Day 1 – Set the Stage

Last week, we learned the fruit of the Tree of the Knowledge of Good and Evil is deadly. This week let's discover how by increasing our understanding of the progression of sin.

Read James 1:13-15. What is the progression of sin?

____

____

____

The progression James describes tells us sin does not begin with the act; it begins in our minds. Like a train speeding along on a track, the more we entertain thoughts which don't line up with God's Word, the faster we go down a deadly track. If we don't stop the thoughts, we go racing into deadly territory and crash into an action that brings us harm. We can't see sin from the outside at the point it becomes sin. To overcome our sinful desires, we must develop a hunger for God and His wisdom and keep that hunger stirred up by having our minds constantly renewed to the Word of God. If we don't, we will find ourselves separated from Him before we even realize it.

The TKGE produces shame and victimization. In the Garden, after his sin, when Adam answered God he admitted, "I was afraid because I was naked." When God asked, "Who told you that you were naked?" Adam replied, "'Yes,' adding, 'but it was the woman you gave me who brought me the fruit…'" When God asked Eve about it, she replied, "The serpent tricked me, that's why I ate it" (Genesis 3:10-12).

Day 2 – Focus

Yesterday, in Genesis 3:10-12, we discovered the progression of sin, and watched how Adam and Eve's sin led to shame and victimization. Can you think of a time when sin has led to shame and/or victimization in your life?

____

____

____

Shame causes us to separate ourselves from God so we cannot operate in the freedom Christ has for us. It is a veil that comes between God and us. Shame covers us completely, even our eyes, so we can see only dimly who and where God is.

God said to Adam and Eve, "Who told you that you were naked?" His tone was most likely similar to one of sadness and angst. God knew they had eaten from the Tree of Knowledge of Good and Evil and it had polluted them. Shame causes us to do all sorts of things that keep us from connecting with God. Shame is when we want to hide. Is there something in your life right now causing you to want to hide?

____

____

____

Prior to eating the forbidden fruit, Adam and Eve were naked and NOT ashamed (Genesis 2:25). Afterward they tried to hide from God's presence in the trees of the garden. They felt they no longer had value and could not come to God honestly. How often do we do the same?

When we sin and try to hide, we are concentrating on our sin instead of concentrating on our Savior.

Why is shame so deadly?

____

____

____

Shame strips us of the power to change. It keeps us from receiving the provision God made for our sin through the blood of Jesus. Shame is unique from guilt. Guilt is based in what we have done, but shame is founded in who we are. With guilt, there is always the opportunity for a fresh start, but with shame, we are trapped because the problem stays with us. With shame, we are the problem, and the ONLY solution is seeing ourselves as God sees us.

Read Psalm 103:11-13 and 1 John 1:9. When are we to have shame and why?

____

Have you ever been overcome by shame?

____

What steps should you take to remove the barrier of shame from your life?

____

What does God promise in these verses?

____

Day 4 - Reflect

Victimization is a natural response to our sin and shame. It is the reason we see Adam and Eve say, "The devil made me do it; the woman you gave me made me do it." We blame others and ourselves by displacing responsibility. We get into condemnation thinking. In blaming others, we look at everything in terms of right and wrong. We say, "If everybody would just live like they are supposed to, everything would work out right." We notice other's sins, but not our own or we blame ourselves by saying, "I'll never be good enough." Whether we blame others or ourselves with victimization, we feel we are powerless to change! It's the reason victimization is so deadly! Where have you taken on a "victim mentality" in your life?

Read John 8:1-11. With shame and victimization, we're either the Pharisee or the woman caught in adultery. How should you change your way of thinking regarding the situation you mentioned above?

We are either basing our lives on our relationship with God or on our relationship with others and our works. We must get to a point where, no matter what happens, we take responsibility for our own lives. We can't blame anyone else for our level of relationship with God! The fruit of the Tree of the Knowledge of Good and Evil lacks the power to transform the heart. It only provides facts and information, but it is powerless to give us life. The TKGE is counterfeit to a relationship with God. Our identity is not based on our own efforts, but on the finished work of Jesus.

Day 5 – Journal: Affirmations

Let's journal our affirmations, thoughts, and prayers, based on what we have learned this week. Don't forget to include any truths God has taught you and what He wants you to do with your new found understanding. Close your time in a prayer of thanksgiving for His great love for you even when you sin or feel shame.

Here's an affirmation to get you started.

My identity is not based on my own efforts, but on the finished work of Jesus.

Week 13: The Tree of Life (TOL) – Fruits of the TOL

Day 1 – Set the Stage

We've discovered much about the Tree of Knowledge of Good and Evil (TKGE), including how its fruit leads to shame and victimization. Now, let's turn our focus to the Tree of Life (TOL) and its fruits which can set us free from wrong thoughts not only about ourselves but also about God.

Read Galatians 5:13. What is our calling as believers?

____

____

As Christ followers, we need to train, building up our faith by reading God's Word and training our thoughts to line up with Biblical truths. It is here that Tree of Life thinking comes into play, helping us to learn how to truly live in the freedom we are promised in Christ.

Read Psalm 119:105. What do we know about God's Word from this passage?

____

____

It's really simple – God's Word lights the way for us, allowing us to approach every situation we encounter, but we have to be in His Word daily to get the positive effects! God's commands aren't intended to be burdensome to us, but rather a part of His divine plan to protect us from danger and give us success in Him. As we continue our quest to better ourselves, we will grow closer to Him, hear His voice clearly, and find His heart for us!

Day 2 - Focus

Write out Matthew 11:28-30. What is true freedom in Christ?

____

____

____

Living in the Tree of Life bring us fellowship with God and true freedom in Christ.

Read John 17:3. What is the promise of eternal life?

____

____

The word "know" in this verse is the Greek word _ginosko_ and it means to recognize, to understand, or to understand completely. It indicates a relationship in which each person is of value and importance. The way – the only way – we can experience the abundant life God wants for us is by truly knowing Him.

Read 1 John 4:9-10. What do you learn about real love?

____

____

He invites us to love Him, but only after His lavish display of love for us through the sacrifice of Jesus. God loves us so much, He made a blood covenant which cannot be broken – with His Son, Jesus to make a way for us to be in a relationship with Him (Hebrews 6:17-18). Unlike the Old Testament Covenants God made with man and man messed them up – this covenant cannot be broken which means nothing can separate us from His love!

Day 3 – Foundation

Read Genesis 2:25. What do you learn about Adam and Eve?

____

Read Genesis 3:7. What has changed? Why?

____

From our earlier study, we know they had sinned, eating from the Tree of the Knowledge of Good and Evil. They had broken fellowship with God. Think about this – as we spend time walking with God, hearing His voice, talking to Him, obeying Him, worshipping Him, and enjoying our relationship with Him, we are transformed on the outside and within is as well. We become, in a sense, "naked" – transparent and unashamed before Him. Nakedness here speaks of innocence. In Genesis 2, Adam and Eve were unaware of any reason to hide from God. They had no sin consciousness. Little ones running about with no clothes after a bath comes to mind, their childlike innocence an amazing virtue.

For Adam and Eve, nakedness was part of the innocence and simplicity of their lives. They were clothed in the glory of God. Before they sinned, they had nothing of which to be ashamed. It is the concept Jesus spoke of in Matthew 19:14 when He said we had to be like little children to enter the Kingdom of Heaven. God wants us to be mature in our thinking, but for God to work in us in power, childlikeness must be an ingredient (Matthew 10:16, I Corinthians 14:20). Good works cannot produce innocence and fellowship with God but innocence and fellowship with God produces good works. Innocence is born out of a friendship with God.

Read the passages below and note what you learn about living as child of God.

Matthew 5:39-44

____

____

Luke 6:27-36

____

____

In these passages, Jesus tells us how to live as children of God, in both innocence and freedom. Using these scriptures, can you describe what living in innocence looks like?

____

____

Paul warns in 2 Corinthians 11:3, "But I fear that somehow your pure and undivided devotion to Christ will be corrupted, just as Eve was deceived by the cunning ways of the serpent." When we live in the Tree of Life, our focus changes from our sins and shortcomings to God and His goodness. God restores our innocence – a conduit of His power. When we are filled with the Holy Spirit and abide in Jesus, we become free from the works of darkness in our lives. We become vessels of honor useful to God. His life will flow through us, and there will be nothing we cannot do! Innocence keeps our minds and hearts pure so we can see and understand God. As we see God and submit our lives to Him, we become equipped for every good work (2 Timothy 3:17).

Day 5 – Journal – Affirmations

As we close our week, let's journal our affirmations, thoughts, and prayers, based on what we have learned. Include what God has taught you, what He wants you to do in light of His teaching, or compose a simple prayer of thanks, guidance, praise, or requests.

Instead of our usual affirmation to get started, let's do something different this week. Rewrite Acts 10:38, replacing your name where Jesus' name is and your city where you read the word Nazareth. Read it aloud. The power of God will equip you for every good work.

____

____

____

____

____

____

____

____

____

____

____

Week 14: The Tree of Life – Living in the TOL

Day 1 – Set the Stage

"So now there is no condemnation for those who belong to Christ Jesus. For the power of the life-giving Spirit has freed you through Christ Jesus from the power of sin that leads to death" (Romans 8:1-2).

As believers, chosen to be God's adopted children, we need to fully understand how to live in the Tree of Life.

Read Romans 12:1-3. What do you learn is required for living in the Tree of Life?

____

____

____

In Tree of Life living, we can be free from bondage in our thoughts, our actions, and our relationships with God and people. This week, let's look at some powerful truths which can help us form a firm foundation and build a life in Christ that is abundant and free. We have to move out of the shadow of the Tree of the Knowledge of Good and Evil and into the light of the Tree of Life. To do so, we have to not only know who Jesus is but also who we are because of Him. It begins with by being "transformed by the renewing of our minds."

Living in the Tree of Life requires a relationship with the Father. As humans, our right relationship with God was severed when Adam sinned. Jesus restored the relationship through the cross but to enjoy it, we must receive His extravagant love for us expressed in Romans 5:8, "While we were still sinners, Christ died for us."

Day 2 - Focus

Because of Christ's finished work on the cross, we are righteous before God. Read Romans 5:1. What is promised?

According to this verse we have been justified through faith, our right relationship with God is restored and we have peace. We do not serve God out of duty or fear like a servant who has an obligation to be faithful or suffer the consequences.

Read Galatians 4:7 and 2 Corinthians 6:18. How are you living your life – as a servant or as a son or daughter?

As God's sons and daughters, we serve because we are part of the family, we are faithful because of our love for our Father in heaven. Much like our earthly relationships are strengthened with time and fellowship, our relationship with God becomes stronger and more meaningful as we spend time with Him in prayer, read His Word, and fellowship with other believers. In the Tree of Life, we realize doing so is a result of our relationship with Him. Falling in love with Him transforms duty to devotion. Choosing daily to live in the Tree of Life in every circumstance and responding to every situation with godliness is crucial to walking in freedom with Him. God desires that we live life His way – the only way to produce Godly fruit.

Day 3 - Foundation

In Matthew 11, Jesus compares His way of living to the religious Pharisees way of life. The Pharisees were legalistic and self-righteous. Their approach to God was in the strict keeping of all Jewish laws.

Read Matthew 11:28-30 again. What is Jesus's response to the heavy burden that comes from trying to keep the law?

____

____

Read Deuteronomy 30:19. Here, Moses challenged the Israelites to choose the path they would follow - one led to death, the other led to life. What are you choosing? To live in the TKGE or the TOL? Do your daily decisions bring life to those around you?

____

____

____

____

____

Each of us need to ask the Lord to help us make life-giving decisions every day. How? We should start the day with prayer. Then, throughout the day, when we are faced with a difficult decision or situation, we need to pause, examine our motives, and ask Him for wisdom. By retraining the way we think and respond, though it takes time, we can learn and grow in our successes and our failures.

Day 4 - Reflect

Read Romans 12:2. What is the reminder for us here? Why is it so important to our freedom, to living in the Tree of Life?

____

____

____

This verse tells us to renew our minds to the truth of the Word of God. Real change happens when we know the Word of God and what it says. Many times we allow our worldview and past experiences shape our version of truth. We can never make the Bible line up to our version of truth, but we can line up our truth with the Bible. Changing our internal truth will change our external responses. In order to do it, we must be daily in His Word. The pattern of this world leads to death, but God's will lead to life!

Read 2 Corinthians 10:5. What can we do?

____

____

We can examine every thought and action for godly accuracy. If it does not line up with what the Bible says, we must take it captive and make it obedient to the Word of God. As we put God's Word ahead of our feelings and beliefs, it will become a way of life. We can't just read the Bible, we have to, as Paul says in Ephesians 4, let the Holy Spirit renew our thoughts and our attitudes and to put on our new self which is created in the very likeness of God in righteousness and holiness." It is a choice we must make to renew our thoughts, attitudes, and beliefs God's Way.

Day 5 – Journal – Affirmations

As we close our week, let's journal our affirmations, thoughts, and prayers, based on what we have learned. Include what God has taught you, what He wants you to do in light of His teaching, or compose a simple prayer of thanks, guidance, praise, or requests. Here's a prayer based on Philippians 4:8 to get you started.

God, help me to fix my thoughts on what is true, and honorable, and right, and pure, and lovely, and admirable. Help me to think about the things which are excellent and worthy of praise.

____

____

____

____

____

____

____

____

____

____

Week 15: Spiritual Order – Submission is NOT What You Think

Day 1 – Set the Stage

To live daily in the Tree of Life, we need to know two things. First, God designed us with three distinct parts, and second, we need to embrace the principles of spiritual order. Understanding these truths will help us walk in pathways of righteousness. As His creation, we long to live in fellowship with God, but since Adam and Eve's original sin, we have battled with our sin nature. We desire to be holy, but it is not natural for us.

Write out Romans 7:21-23. How does Paul explain the struggle?

____

____

____

Paul explains the internal struggle we all experience. The desire to do what is right (obedience/submission to God) wars with our propensity to do wrong (sin against God).

Read 1 Thessalonians 5:23. God designed us with three distinct parts which can help us live God's Way (in the Tree of Life). Based on this verse, what are those parts?

____

____

We see three unique parts: spirit, soul, and body. At the moment of salvation, our spirit is made alive in Christ and put in right standing with God (Romans 3:24, 5:1) but the soul and body require additional time to conform to the image of Christ (Ephesians 4:12-13).

Day 2 – Focus

When our spirit is made alive in Christ and we enter into right standing with God – the Bible calls the process justification (just-as-if-I-had-never-sinned). The conforming of our soul and body to the image of Christ is a gradual process known as sanctification. God desires for us to be transformed into His image with ever-increasing glory. We must learn to hear His voice and be led by His Spirit. Because we possess a spirit which must be redeemed, a soul which must be restored, and a body which must learn to submit (2 Corinthians 3:16-18).

Read Galatians 4:19. How does Paul describe the process of sanctification?

____

____

Paul tells us about the process of sanctification, like labor pains, but how long it takes depends on how we engage with the Word of God, how quickly we understand it as absolute truth, and how diligently we apply it to all of our circumstances.

Read Colossians 2:13-14. What was the price God paid for this reconciliation?

____

____

The blood of Jesus was the price God paid so we could be reconciled back to Him. In fact, we were designed as spiritual beings with a temporary physical experience on earth, NOT as physical beings with a temporary spiritual experience. It ensures our relationship with God. God's plan is for our spirit to be the strongest of our three part design, to be the "command center" of all we are and all we do.

Day 3 - Foundation

It is pretty amazing, isn't it? From the moment we are saved, we are made alive in Christ, forever redeemed and made righteous before the Father. We not only receive the incredible gift of eternal life in Christ, we also receive the Holy Spirit and gain the ability to be in a relationship with God immediately. The cross of Christ bridges the chasm of death and provides a way for us to have fellowship, communication, and access to the Tree of Life. Like a bride and groom are joined in marriage and become one; our spirit and the Spirit of Christ are united and become one at the moment of salvation.

Write 1 Corinthians 6:17.

____

How does knowing our spirit is redeemed and is in right standing with the Father change the way we know ourselves?

____

____

Because we are one with Christ, we have the ability to understand spiritual truths and discern right from wrong. We are able to hear the voice of God and adjust accordingly. Sometimes there may be static (distraction, fear, confusion, etc.), like when searching for a radio station but if we continue to seek the Lord and His way of living, our spirit can rise above the static and we can tune into the broadcast of truth. Even so, God created our souls with the capacity to think, reason, and express emotions – He even gave us the ability to choose.

Day 4 – Reflect

In Genesis 2:7, God formed our bodies from the earth. The body acts as a temporary house or shell and contains our soul and spirit (1 Corinthians 6:19). Our bodies are specially designed by God, given to us to carry out the plans He has for us. When we live a life surrendered to Him (living in the Tree of Life, God's way) we aren't looking for loop-holes in His law, but instead we are falling more and more in love with Him and His plan for our life.

Our bodies have many appetites, good and bad. The Bible warns us to be careful of sin which allows our flesh to get anything it wants. As humans we often wonder, "How far can I sin and still enjoy the benefits of God's blessing?" The trap – sin NEVER satisfies. Instead it leaves us always looking to fulfill the next craving and gain momentary satisfaction only to return with increased intensity as the cycle builds and repeats itself. The cycle can only be broken by the power of the Holy Spirit.

Are your actions being driven by your cravings?

____

Read 1 Corinthians 6:12. Why is doing anything we are allowed not a good idea?

____

____

We belong to Jesus. He purchased not only our freedom but our life with His blood. We need to filter our actions with this question: "How will this action affect those around me?" By reviewing the consequences of our sin beforehand, we can more easily submit to God and live in the Tree of Life, experiencing the abundant life He has for us.

Day 5 - Journal - Affirmations

As we close our week, let's journal any affirmations, thoughts, and prayers, based on what we have learned. This week note not only affirmations but also answer the question: "What did God teach you this week about the war going on inside you and how to overcome it?"

Here's an affirmation from this week to help you get started.

Not everything is good for me. I should not allow myself to become a slave to anything.

Week 16: Spiritual Order – Walking in the Spirit (Ordered Living)
Day 1 – Set the Stage

As we continue our efforts to live in freedom, this week we'll explore how to walk in the Spirit as we learn the concept of ordered living. Spiritual order provides the framework we need to live in the Tree of Life - living with our spirits united with God and our souls and bodies submitted to our spirits. It means our spirit (now one with God through salvation in Christ) is in command with our souls and bodies following the spirit's lead. Sounds good right? But the question remains, "If we are saved, why do we continue to struggle with sin?"

____

____

The answer is found in the sanctification process and the spiritual order principle. Read 2 Peter 1:3. Once we are saved, do we have what we need to live a godly life?

____

____

The answer is yes, but we still struggle. Why? Our spirit is not in the lead. So, how do we get our spirit to take the lead? The area we give the most attention will become the most influential in our lives, which means we have to feed our spirit more than our body or soul. The "world" feeds our soul through everything we see and hear. Our bodies, if hungry, don't hesitate to let us know. In fact, when we withhold gratification from our souls and bodies, they get loud! Our spirit, when not fed, gets quiet. We have to be intentional to feed our spirit. What are you doing to feed your spirit?

Day 2 – Focus

Of our three distinct parts – spirit, soul, and body – which is in control? The soul and the body are complex and often confusing, especially since we are used to them taking the lead.

Very early in our lives, we learn to take instruction from our souls. Every one of us had seen a toddler throw himself on the floor and demand his own way. He is being led by his emotions. The same is true when he holds his breath until his parent gives in to his demands.

We'd like to think this only happens in the lives of children, but we all know adults possess the same tendencies. Have you ever heard someone say, "If it feels good, do it" or "I don't feel like doing that?" These examples are the epitome of a soul-led life.

Read Galatians 5:19-21 and list the works of the soul-led life.

____

____

Read Galatians 6:8. What is the result of living a life that gratifies the body?

____

____

What happens when a person lives a spirit-led life?

____

____

Spirit, soul, or body – which is in control of your life?

Day 3 – Foundation

Read Galatians 5:22-23. What fruit is produced in us when we live spirit-led lives?

____

____

____

Living a spirit-led life, we see love, joy, peace, patience, kindness, goodness, faithfulness, gentleness, and self-control manifest in our lives. Living in spiritual order brings incredible benefits, such as protection, spiritual growth, and power to overcome obstacles in our lives.

It is dangerous to live outside of spiritual order. When we choose to do things our way, our lifestyle opens the door for the enemy to operate freely in our lives and we forgo the protection and safety God has promised when we live spirit-led lives.

Read Psalm 91. Looking at verses 9-12, who is afforded the benefits of protection and safety? What is promised?

____

____

____

____

There is protection from the enemy when we choose to live life God's way, giving Him control over our lives.

Day 4 - Reflect

We all want to live life God's way, but what happens when we fall short or give in to temptation?

____

In those times, we distance ourselves from God. We feel shame and condemnation, but we know that's TKGE thinking. God doesn't bring condemnation but rather conviction. Godly sorrow for our sin leads us to repentance and allows us to turn away from sin.

Read Psalm 66:18-20. What do we need to do when we fall short? What is promised when we do?

____

____

____

When we're out of spiritual order, we need to stop and repent. We need to ask for AND receive His grace. The kindness of the Lord leads us to repentance (Romans 2:4).

Every single day we face decisions, and our choices dictate our lives. How do we make good decisions?

____

We need to understand our identity in Christ (2 Corinthians 5:17), change the way we think (Romans 12:2), and be led by the Spirit. Think about who you are in Him and seek the power of the Holy Spirit to live life walking with Jesus.

Day 5 – Journal: Affirmations

As we close our week, let's take a few minutes to write Ephesians 1:4.

____

____

____

Now rewrite it as today's affirmation as you journal affirmations, thoughts, and prayers.

Week 17: God Can Be Trusted – Heart Blockages

Day 1 – Set the Stage

Read Titus 2:11-12. What did God bring to the peoples of the world? When we accept His gift of salvation, how does it help us live in our world?

____

____

____

Jesus came not only to give us life, but a rich abundant life which overflows into the lives of those around us. But just how do we achieve that life practically? This powerful kind of living requires us to totally surrender our lives to Christ. It begins with forgiveness – a type of surrender and a condition for walking in the fullness of all God offers us.

As we start speaking the Word of God over our lives, power is released to us (the same power that raised Jesus from the dead) and our lives begin to manifest changes of which we had only dreamed possible. What kind of changes? (Hint: reread the verse above)

____

____

____

With Christ as our Savior we can break through our heart blockages, turn from godless living and sinful pleasures, and live our lives with wisdom, righteousness, and devotion to God.

Day 2 – Focus

Surrendering our heart, our relationships, and our possessions to God makes us step outside our comfort zones, but as we grow in our relationship with Him, we realize He is a God who we can trust. As we release all things to God, we give Him permission to intervene on our behalf in every aspect of our lives. In like manner, we also come to understand those things to which we hold so tightly become our responsibility.

Read Hebrews 4:11. What are we instructed to do?

This verse tells us to strive to enter into the rest of God, but we know we cannot rest while carrying the burdens of this world. Our ability to rest in the Lord is spiritual warfare which requires us to obey God's command to forgive others. When we release those who have hurt us to the Lord, we support the truth that His grace is enough.

We can't sacrifice spiritual order for justice; the cost is too great! Forgiving ourselves is necessary in order that we can forgive others and live in the Tree of Life. Nothing changes our spiritual lives quite as much as understanding the power of words. We are accountable for the words we use because the spoken word is powerful. Can you think of a time when you changed your circumstances by changing your words?

Day 3 – Foundation

Read Proverbs 4:20-23. What makes our words so important?

____

What are we instructed to do regarding our hearts? Why?

____

Read 1 Samuel 16:7. Where does God focus His attention?

____

Given the importance of our hearts, let's read the following verses and uncover the four blockages of our hearts mentioned in each passage.

James 3:14-15

____

Luke 17:1, Proverbs 18:19

____

Proverbs 18:21

____

Mark 7:21

____

Envy, selfish ambition, disorder, temptations, arguments, evil thoughts, and all evils come from within, blocking our hearts to God's best for us – abundant life. We must get rid of our heart blockages for our hearts determine the course of our lives.

Day 4 – Reflect

In order to speak Words of Life, we must understand what the Word of God says about surrender and forgiveness.

Are there areas of your life you have not surrendered to the Lord?

____

Why are you holding on to them?

____

What would you lose by letting go?

____

What would you gain?

____

Have you ever thought about your words having power?

____

Do you speak words of life? Words of death?

____

We know our hearts determine the course of our lives. We stay in spiritual order by feeding our spirit – not our soul or our body. Ask God to show you areas of your life which you have not surrendered. Ask Him to help you surrender, forgive, and trust Him with your whole heart. Ask God to enlighten you regarding the connection between the words you speak and the condition of your heart. Ask Him to help you speak words of life over you, your family, and your circumstances.

Day 5 - Journal: Affirmations

As we close our week, let's take a few minutes to journal our affirmations, thoughts, and prayers, based on what we have learned. A journal is also a good way to record the faithfulness of God and help you to document a history with God. This week ask God to help you not only with areas of your life which you have surrendered, but also those areas which are harder to surrender.

God, help me to guard my heart above all else, because it determines the course of my life.

Week 18: God Can Be Trusted – Transforming the Heart

Day 1 – Set the Stage

We serve a God who can be trusted, a loving God who longs to transform our hearts. Read Ezekiel 36:26-27. What does God promise?

____

____

____

____

____

Earlier in Ezekiel, we see Israel's heart was steeped in rebellion and idolatry. In spite of the covenant they had broken with Him, despite their hardened hearts against Him, God, in His infinite grace, promised them a New Covenant, an unconditional one, a covenant without conditions or requirements they could break.

The New Covenant described in these verses was one in which the Lord promised a new heart to His people, one that is not hardened against Him but instead sensitive to Him and His Word.

His promise was fulfilled through the nation of Israel, through the Messiah who would come. Today, in the 21st Century, we know the New Covenant was fulfilled by Jesus Christ and those who believe are the beneficiaries of God's promises – a new heart and a new mind. Through Him, we, as His followers, can carry out His plan through the power of His Spirit living in us. Through Him, all our heart blockages can be removed and our hearts can be transformed.

Day 2 - Focus

Read Psalm 139:23-24. How then are our hearts transformed?

____

____

____

The transformation process begins when we invite the Holy Spirit into our lives to examine our hearts and enlighten us so we can confess our sin and be better able to follow and serve the Lord. In these verses, David is asking God to give him a repentant heart so that he can truly be a man after God's "own heart" as he would later be described.

The Hebrew word translates as heart in this passage is *levav* and it is used to refer to thoughts and intentions as well as resolve and courage. When David asks God into his heart and mind, he is asking God to help him see things the way God sees them so he can follow God's leading for His life.

David also asks God to know his "anxious thoughts." What do you think he means?

____

____

We all have anxious thoughts, those which arise from our disbelief or lack of trust in God, and God is the only one who can remedy those thoughts, turning us back to His way, reminding us that He can be trusted.

Read Psalm 51:10-12. Our transformation continues when we invite the Holy Spirit to do what in our lives?

In this Psalm, in these verses, David is asking God to cleanse his heart, to renew his spirit. What does he mean? After all, if we have accepted Christ's gift of salvation, God has forgiven our sins - past, present, and future.

What David is asking is much deeper, based more in the consequences of sin, even though they are forgiven. It is a prayer of remorse, repentance, and renewal.

David penned this Psalm after his sin with Bathsheba (adultery) and the murder of her husband Uriah to cover it up. After a visit from Nathan the prophet, David realized the extent of his sin, his complete betrayal of God. In these verses, David is crying out for God's mercy, but also a radical cleansing, and full restoration. He is asking God to intervene, to redirect his thoughts and his heart. Finally David asks God to restore his joy and give him an obedient heart. David didn't want to live life going through the motions. He wanted the unspeakable joy which can only come from a heart that is right with God, a heart unabashedly obedient to the Father.

Day 4 - Reflect

Read Ephesians 5:18. What is the final step toward a truly transformed heart?

____

____

____

To complete our transformation, we must invite the Holy Spirit to fill us so that we do not seek our pleasure and fulfillment in worldly pursuits or possessions. In Paul's letter to the believers, he explains who we are in Christ - our redemption, our reconciliation, and our transformation. He continues, describing the indwelling of the Holy Spirit in us. In this passage, Paul is in the middle of a discussion of how we are to live as mature believers when he admonishes, "Do not get drunk on wine, which leads to debauchery. Instead, be filled with the Spirit." Being filled with the Spirit is not a one-time event, but an ongoing filling which needs to take place daily.

In God's Word, filling means to be "ruled, controlled, or under submission." As believers, we are to be submitted to the Holy Spirit, controlled by Him, following His leadership in every aspect of our lives.

What are we warned against?

____

____

Specifically being drunk with wine, but generally anything which might control us to the point that we dishonor God. We are to let the Holy Spirit fill us daily so that in all we do we bring glory and honor to God and lead others to salvation in Him.

Day 5 – Journal – Affirmations

As we close our week, let's journal what we've learned about God and also about our own heart. Are their steps we need to take toward our total transformation? Are we letting the Holy Spirit fill us daily or are other "things" filling us? Note what God has taught you and what He wants you to do in light of His teaching.

Lord help me to be filled with the Holy Spirit daily, always ready to serve you.

Week 19: Surrender – Surrender Requires Trust
Day 1 – Set the Stage

When you think surrender what comes to mind?

____

____

The word surrender brings much to mind, from a white flag waving over a ship to a platoon of soldiers with hands raised and guns at their feet. We often associate surrender with defeat but in God's Word surrender takes on a whole new meaning. When it comes to a life with Christ, surrendering our control over our lives is the first step toward true freedom.

Read Proverbs 3:5-6. What are we instructed to do? What is the reward?

____

____

A life of surrender and submission requires trust. In turn, trust is developed in the context of relationship. Trust is earned, which means until we gain an understanding of a person's character, we aren't likely to trust him or her with anything of value. In order to surrender to God, we have to believe He is worthy of our trust. Sadly, it is often difficult to do because of our doubts or past disappointments with people or churches. Our hearts may be hardened, but we have hope! When we understand what Jesus did for us - left heaven for earth; felt hurt and rejection; was beaten and crucified; conquered death and rose from the grave - to prove His love, earn our trust and be in a relationship with us, we discover we can trust Him.

Day 2 – Focus

How do we get to know someone better?

____

____

The same is true for God. If we want to know Him better, we do what we would do when getting to know a friend – spend time with Him. It doesn't look the same for everyone. Some of us enjoy walking and talking with friends, others like sitting by the water and chatting. The key is to invite Him into your life and then He will reveal Himself to you as you study His Word, speak with Him in prayer, and grow relationships with other believers.

Read James 4:8. What guidance is here to grow your relationship with God?

____

____

____

Read Isaiah 55:9. What do you learn about God's ways? How can knowing this help you in building your relationship with Him?

____

____

____

God's ways of doing things are different from ours which can make them seem unclear. Yet, when we make the choice to trust Him and obey His Word, we are well on the way to a successful relationship with Him

Day 3 - Foundation

The only way to reach the amazing destinations God has for our lives is to fully surrender to Him and follow His way of life. As we get to know Him, we trust Him more and more, making it easy to surrender to Him. Are there any areas of your life you have not surrendered to God? Is trust the reason?

____

____

God wants to make our lives smoother by being Lord over all. Anything we hold tightly to becomes our responsibility, not His. However, when we surrender all areas of our lives to Him, He partners with us to bring us safely and completely to our final destination. It shouldn't surprise us to learn that a trial with God in charge is smoother than a victory when we are in charge.

Read the following verses and record what Jesus teaches we must surrender to be His disciples.

Luke 14:33

____

Luke 14:26

____

Luke 14:27

____

Genuine surrender is more than devotion. It is giving up to God. When it truly happens, God will meet the needs which resulted from our surrender way better than anything we could have done had we maintained control.

Day 4 – Reflect

We were created to worship. We will always worship what we value most. Read Exodus 20:3-4. What instructions are given to us?

____

____

We are to have no idols. We often think of idols as carved statues, but in reality, idols are anything we value more than God. Idols can be people, jobs, sports, hobbies, etc. – those things which are fine to enjoy or admire but aren't worthy of top priority.

Read Matthew 6:33. What should we worship and give top priority in our lives?

____

____

God must be first. When we are consumed with "things" we are materialistic and become victims to the pressure to have more! It is then that we give the enemy the opening he seeks to attack our hearts and minds with incessant thoughts about what we have and how much more we want. Think about it – the more we have, the more attention and care we have to give it.

Is there anything in your life that is more important than God?

____

Surrender it now to Him. Take heed to His admonition and trust His promise in Hebrews 13:5 "Don't love money; be satisfied with what you have. For God has said, 'I will never fail you. I will never abandon you.'"

Day 5 – Journal – Affirmations

As we close our week, let's journal about what God taught us about surrender, what we surrendered, and what God wants us to do going forward. Here's an affirmation to get you started.

God will never fail me. God will never abandon me.

Week 20: Surrender – How to Surrender All

Day 1 - Set the Stage

Did you know relationships can come between you and God, much like the "things" we talked about last week? It's true, relationships can become idols to which we attach more importance than our relationship with God.

Read Genesis 22:1-18. What does God ask Abraham to do?

____

____

____

For most of us, this is a seemingly inconceivable situation. Abraham had waited decades for God to fulfill the promise that he would be the father of nations. Finally in Abraham's old age, God blessed him with a son, Isaac. Abraham is overjoyed as the child grows, but then one day, God tells Abraham to sacrifice the boy on an altar. We know Abraham had questions. We know he loved Isaac very much - but he also trusted God. He got up early the next morning to obey God. He didn't delay; he didn't try to find a way out. With great faith, he placed Isaac on the altar and set out to follow God's command, had an angel not stopped him. God saw Abraham's obedience, provided an alternate sacrifice, and blessed him with a family heritage unlike any other.

Abraham walked in submission to God and clearly he could hear the voice of the Lord. Like Abraham, God's blessing can flow from us to every relationship we have if we readily surrender them to Him. Where do your relationships stand? Do you have a relationship that has come between you and God?

Day 2 – Focus

There are many areas of our lives which we need to surrender to God. They may include relationships or things but also plans, goals, pleasures, ambitions, hurts, the future, the past, selfishness, ego, sin, pride, physical appearance, lust, anger, fear, and health. Even unforgiveness can fall under the category of "self," because holding on to an offense is essentially saying we have a right to withhold grace from someone. This type of pride is an idol which causes a wedge between God and us.

Surrendering does not mean we must have no goals or ambitions. On the contrary, God is the One who puts those desires in our hearts. Surrender doesn't mean our personality has to drastically change or we need to become someone else. However, it does mean we submit ourselves to His will and join with Him in His plans for us.

Read Romans 12:9-19. List the actions you read.

____

____

____

____

Don't pretend, really love others. Hate what is wrong. Stand on the side of the good. Love and honor one another. Don't be lazy, serve the Lord enthusiastically. Be glad for all God is planning for you. Be patient. Be prayerful. Help others. Pray for those who persecute you. Be happy for others' happiness. Share others' sorrow. Live harmoniously. Don't act important, like you know it all. Never pay back evil for evil. Act honorably. Live at peace with others. Don't take revenge.

How would your life change if you lived this way?

____

Day 3 – Foundation

What allows us to have truly godly relationships?

____

____

Godly relationships happen when we stay free of offense. The most difficult relationships to surrender may be the ones where there is offense and unforgiveness.

What if you gave up your "right to be right" and instead chose to be unoffended no matter the situation?

____

____

We can learn to remain unoffended as we study the life of Jesus and study God's Word. Read Colossians 3:17, 23-25. How can we live a life without offense?

____

____

____

____

____

Be thankful. Be aware of God's provision and blessing. Don't try to control others; let them make their own decisions as God allows you to make yours. Make decisions which promote life. When someone offends you, speak up as Jesus did, in love, and act appropriately. Trust God for justice. Give grace. Live your life as if everything you do is for the Lord – because ultimately it is!

Day 4 – Reflect

Have you surrendered your past, present, and future to God? What makes you say that?

____

____

Do you trust His way is better than your own? Why?

____

____

Many years ago John Henry Sammis wrote the lyrics to a now famous hymn, "Trust and Obey" The lyrics proclaim, "Trust and obey for there's no other way / To be happy in Jesus, but to trust and obey." Those two words, "trust" and "obey" sum up what it means to surrender.

As we walk through this life, things and people will try to take the lead in our lives and capture the number one spot on our list. Surrendering daily keeps us walking down the right path. Read Isaiah 30:21. When we trust and obey, surrendering to God daily, we are the recipients of God's promise of love, compassion, help, and guidance. What is promised in this verse when surrender daily?

____

____

We won't turn to the right or to the left because of distractions or temptations because we will hear the voice of the Lord saying, "This is the pathway, walk in it" and we will have the power within to do so.

Day 5 – Journal – Affirmations

As we close our week, let's take a few minutes to journal not only our affirmations, thoughts, and prayers, but also what we have learned about surrender. Include what God has taught you specifically and what He wants you to do in response to His teaching.

Here's an affirmation to get you started.

When I surrender to God, I can be His representative in all that I do or say.

Week 21: Forgiveness – Are You Harboring Unforgiveness?

Day 1 – Set the Stage

Let's begin this week by reading Isaiah 1:18. What matter is settled in this verse and how is it settled?

____

____

____

Our sins, though they are many, are forgiven, washed away by the blood of Christ.

There is no doubt, we live in a fallen world, because we face the realities of hurt and offense daily. The words and deeds of others wound us in indescribable ways. We experience neglect, abuse, violence, betrayal, and cruel remarks which cause bitterness and resentment to infiltrate our hearts, and although it may not be our intention, unforgiveness results.

An offense laced with unforgiveness can be like an arrow tipped in poison. The offense slashes through our defenses in the moment and hurts us. The aftermath is unforgiveness which remains after the event takes place. It's like bitter poison as it seeps into us, tainting our thoughts and clouding our vision. If we don't do something, it will penetrate our hearts and paralyze us. When someone does wrong to us, unforgiveness often feels like the right response, but the truth is harboring unforgiveness is much like drinking poison and expecting the offending person to die. It just doesn't work that way!

Are you harboring unforgiveness?

Unforgiveness keeps us in bondage and prevents us from living the abundant life God desires for us. Why do you think it is so hard to forgive others?

We have the wrong idea about forgiveness. Forgiveness doesn't mean minimizing the offense. It's not saying to the one who committed the wrong, "Oh, it's no big deal." When we are hurt, it is a big deal because it caused us pain. What was said or done wasn't right and the hurt or harm we felt does not reflect the Father's heart for us. God's perfect will is to protect and nurture us.

When we choose to forgive, we choose to let go of the offense because if we don't, we are robbed of our freedom. Letting go of the offense does not mean we must reconcile with the person. Forgiveness is not reconciliation.

Read Romans 12:18. What does this verse imply?

God understands there are times when reconciliation may not be the best choice. The offender may not be ready to reconcile and attempting to do will only cause us further pain and disappointment. We have to let the Holy Spirit lead us as we allow the miracle of forgiveness to happen.

Day 3 - Foundation

Read Matthew 6:14-15 and Colossians 3:13. What do you learn about forgiveness?

____

____

____

We offer forgiveness to others so we can be free. For our relationships to be restored, the offender must:

- Repent – Turn away from wrong actions and go in the opposite direction

- Offer Restitution – Make things right if possible

- Rebuild Trust - Prove themselves consistent in words and actions

We often tell ourselves, "When they apologize, I will forgive them" but by choosing this path, we become the hostage to the one who wronged us because it leaves our freedom in the hands of the offender. Reconciliation requires two players – the offender and the offended, but forgiveness only requires one.

Forgiveness is not forgetting. "Forgive and forget" is a cliché without truth. We don't need to forget in order to forgive because in truth we may never forget what has happened to us.

God wants to do something extraordinary in our lives – to bring healing to our hearts so we can remember without reliving the pain the offense caused. He wants to show us He can make all things new.

Day 4 – Reflect

We often fail to offer forgiveness because we don't think the ones who hurt us deserve forgiveness – we simply don't think it's fair. Thankfully, God isn't fair because none of us deserves forgiveness.

Read Matthew 18:21-35. What is Jesus trying to convey here?

____

____

____

Jesus uses this parable to explain the profound and undeserved forgiveness extended to us as believers. Jesus told Peter he would need to forgive his brother 490 times a day, or once every three minutes. In the parable, the first man owed a debt of 10,000 talents, equal to about $5 billion today. The master cancelled this debt. Like this man, we, as sinners, owed a great debt we could not pay, but God loves us anyway and through the cross, Jesus paid our debt in full. We are forgiven much.

The second man owed a debt of 100 Denarii, equal to about $10,000 today. It is a significant amount. When someone hurts or offends us, it is significant, but because we have been forgiven much, we can extend what we have received to others.

None of us deserve the forgiveness God has given to us. We should rejoice in the fact that God isn't fair. If He were fair, we would have to pay for our own sins. Thankfully, we don't get what we deserve; instead we have abundant life now and eternal life to come. In light of all we have been forgiven, can we release those who have wronged us?

____

Day 5 – Journal: Affirmations

This has been a difficult week for most of us, as forgiveness is a challenging topic. Many times, we don't forgive because we don't believe we have the strength. As we close our week, write Philippians 4:13.

____

____

Next write 2 Corinthians 12:9.

____

____

____

Consider committing both verses to memory, reminding you of the incredible power of Christ at work in you in the midst of struggles like forgiveness. Forgiveness should not turn us into doormats, instead it gives us victory and freedom in Christ.

Compose a simple prayer asking God to help you as you seek freedom in forgiveness of others.

____

____

____

____

Week 22: Forgiveness – Forgiveness is Vital

Day 1 – Set the Stage

Let's begin this week by reading Ephesians 4:21-32. What are we instructed to do and why?

____

____

____

____

The first step God takes in restoring our relationship with Him is He forgives us. Read Romans 5:18. When did He take that first step?

____

____

He made the first move by choosing to forgive us before we asked! He expects us to make the same decision in all relationships. It is not optional; it is critical. Why? It is impossible to forgive others for their offenses until we receive forgiveness for ourselves. When we struggle with forgiveness, it is probably because we have not fully grasped what has been done for us. When we have difficulty forgiving others, we have not fully understood how large a debt God has forgiven us.

As believers, we have total forgiveness for past, present, and future sin. It is not that God forgets our sins, but rather He chooses to remember our sin no more (Hebrews 8:12). He chooses to never bring up our sin again (Isaiah 43:25). Why? God desperately wants to be in relationship with each of us.

Day 2 – Focus

An offense is a violation of whatever we consider to be right and natural. In Matthew 24:10, Jesus tells us in the last days many will be offended, betray, and hate one another. The Greek word *scandelon* is the word translated as offense, but it actually means "the bait." In Bible times when people wanted to trap an animal a pit would be covered with branches and a piece of flesh (*scandelon*) placed on the pit to lure the animal into the trap. An offense often lures us into the trap of unforgiveness and bondage. Rather than trapping the person who hurt us we are the ones ensnared. Read Proverbs 18:19. What is the progression of offense?

Offense is the bait used by the enemy to lure us into bondage. When offended, we are unyielding, placing walls around our hearts to ensure we are not hurt again. The walls may keep out the bad (pain and hurt), but they also keep out the good (love and healing). We will all face offense in this world – we have to choose not to take the "bait" from the enemy and instead let God protect our hearts.

The enemy uses five common snares to trap us in unforgiveness – betrayed, falsely accused, rejected, abused, or humiliated. Would it surprise you to know Jesus suffered all these offenses while on earth?

Read Hebrews 2:17-18. Why did He need to suffer these offenses?

Jesus experienced all the offenses in a human body so He could understand every struggle we encounter. He overcame and in Him we have the power to do the same.

Read Luke 23:34. This verse is just prior to Jesus death, what can we learn from Him about forgiveness?

____

____

At His death, Jesus asked the Father to forgive the ones who had cursed Him, beaten Him, and nailed His hands and feet to the cross. The secret is not that Jesus was offended, but how he responded to offense. Godly responses to offense keep our hearts pure. They knew exactly what they were doing – killing an innocent man they hated and making sure He felt every ounce of their malice. Jesus chose to see things differently and we can, too. To handle offenses when they come, we must arm ourselves by thinking like Jesus.

Our prayer for people should be that the Lord allows us to see them through the eyes of Jesus. If we can change our viewpoint from worldly to godly, we can love people the way Jesus did (and does) regardless of what they do. How do we keep our hearts pure and unoffended? Read the verses below to answer.

Romans 3:23

____

We need forgiveness and we can never forgive more than God has forgiven us.

1 Peter 5:8

____

We need to focus on the real enemy – the devil. Jesus chose to see the people with the hammer and nails as victims, too. Our goal should be to love people and hate the devil.

1 John 4:10

____

We must receive the love of God which gives us the capacity to love people.

Day 4 – Reflect

The Bible's steps for working out forgiveness are countercultural and counterintuitive but when we follow them, they will change our life.

Read 1 Corinthians 1:25-28. What is the difference between God's plans and humanity's plans?

____

____

____

Our human way of thinking and God's way of thinking are not the same – not even close. Receiving the love of God first is the only way to give it to others. We have to pray for those who have offended us.

The world tells us to return evil for evil, to isolate those who have hurt us so they cannot do it again. Read Matthew 5:43-44. How does Jesus say we should handle it?

____

____

In order to have better results, we have to respond differently than the world expects. How would your life change if you chose to believe the best of everyone?

____

____

For some of us, not talking negatively about those who have wronged us is a huge challenge, but Jesus challenges us to go a step further – to bless those who have wronged us. Who do you need to bless Jesus's way today?

Day 5 – Journal: Affirmations

As we close this week, let's do something a little different. Read Romans 12:17-21 aloud and then write your own declaration/affirmation of freedom and forgiveness from it.

____

____

____

____

____

____

____

Next, for your prayer time today, consider using this prayer of forgiveness to release anyone who has offended you. You can insert the name(s) of those you need to forgive and say the prayer aloud.

> "Lord, I have not loved, but have resented certain people and I have unforgiveness in my heart. Forgive me for my sin of offense. I ask you Lord, to give me the power to release and forgive those who have hurt me. I do now forgive them and ask You to forgive me also. Give me the strength to pray for them, bless them, and want the best for them. Thank you for breaking these chains off my life.

In the name of Jesus I pray, Amen.

Week 23: The Power of Words – Is Your Tongue Selling You Out?

Day 1 - Set the Stage

Earlier this year, we mentioned the power of words and this week we'll go deeper into that truth to find out if our tongues are selling us out!

Read Proverbs 18:21. What do you learn about the tongue?

____

____

____

The words we speak are a spiritual gauge, showing how much of ourselves we have surrendered to God. If our minds have been regularly renewed by the Word, our conversation will reflect what we have learned. If, on the other hand, we are holding on to our old habits and beliefs, our words will betray us, revealing our true spiritual condition. If our souls aren't submitted to God, if we haven't surrendered everything to Him, our tongues will be the first to sell us out.

Read Luke 6:45. What does your day-to-day conversation say about your spiritual condition?

____

____

____

Read Matthew 12:34-35. Do your words reflect God who lives inside of you?

____

____

Day 2 – Focus

Read Matthew 12:36-37. What truth does Jesus share?

____

____

____

Jesus clearly communicates that a life consumed with the treasures of the world will lead to fruitless talk which will, in turn, bring judgment. On the other hand, a life surrendered to God and filled with the Holy Spirit produces speech full of grace, mercy, love, and power.

Read Hebrews 11:13. How does this verse testify to the power of God's Words?

____

____

____

With words, God spoke the universe into being. His Words, recorded in the Bible, are the way He communicates and reveals Himself to us.

Read John 1:1. Who is the Word?

____

It gets even better – Jesus is the living, breathing, Word of God. Words and language were His idea, and His words are life to us. God created man in His image, and so we have the power to speak words of life or words of death. When we speak, we advance the kingdom of life or we advance the kingdom of death. Our words have the power to change our environment.

Why do you think we weren't ushered into heaven when we were saved?

____

____

As Jesus's body — His hands, feet, heart, and mouth — we remain here to reach the lost and make a difference in this world. Jesus understood the pressures we would be under as a result and we would be completely powerless without help. God knew we would not be able to survive the pressures or temptations of the world.

Jesus even told His disciples they would have the advantage if He left and went back to heaven. Read John 16:7. Why did He make that promise?

____

When Jesus returned to heaven, God's incredible plan included leaving us, His followers, the Holy Spirit, who would live inside us and help us to do what sounded impossible - represent Jesus in the world. Jesus, fully God and fully human, could only be in one place while He was on earth in His human body.

Read John 16:13. What does Jesus explain about the Holy Spirit?

____

____

The Holy Spirit lives within us as our personal guide and is with us all the time here on earth which means God discloses to us, by His Spirit, all the guidance we need, including what to say. Are you being intentional in using your words to promote God's kingdom and minister to others?

When our soul is surrendered to God, even our words produce life. In the Garden of Eden, Satan brought death to Eve through his words and she brought death to Adam by repeating Satan's words. From this, we can see the importance of controlling our words.

Read James 3:2-12. What is James teaching?

____

____

Controlling our words requires us to tame a part of ourselves containing the power of life and death: our tongues. We average around 30 conversations a day – what do all those words we use say about us? James argues if we say we are Christians and love God, but our attitudes and actions reflect something different, we may be deceived. In verse 2 James says we can control ourselves in every way if we can control our tongues. Our words tear others down or build them up with encouragement.

Words of life are like salt, bringing out good flavor in conversations and situations. Like the bit used to steer horses, the tongue can control the direction of our lives. The tongue can control us like a rudder controls a ship, or we can use it to control our destiny. Like a spark – abrupt, rude words may be quickly forgotten by the one who said them, but the impact remains. The tongue, like uncontrolled fire, can devour life and cause destruction beyond belief. What words have you been speaking to others? How can God help you speak words of life?

Day 5 - Journal - Affirmations

As we close our week, let's take a few minutes to journal what we have learned about our words. Include what God has taught you personally about your words and what He wants you to do in light of His teaching. Here's an affirmation to get you started.

We were made in God's image, meant to speak words of life that build up, bring healing, and offer encouragement.

Week 24: The Power of Words – Taming the Tongue to Speak Life

Day 1 – Set the Stage

In Matthew 12:34b, we read, "For whatever is in your heart determines what you say." The mouth is going to automatically say what is inside our hearts. It is a truth that might leave us staggering given what we have learned about taming our tongues and training them to speak life. If we truly desire to control our tongues, we need to guard our hearts. In other words, we need to control everything we hear and see, all that junk saturating our souls continually on a daily basis. It is the only way we can become people who speak differently, people who genuinely and regularly speak life.

Read Matthew 12:35. What truth is found here?

____

____

If you've been around a while, you recognize this as the old "garbage in, garbage out" principle, popular in the early days of computing.

Write Psalm 51:10.

____

____

As we begin this week of study on taming the tongue, let's begin with this verse as a prayer for God's help in doing so. Why? We all face negativity on a daily basis, some of us at home, others at school, others still in the workplace, and some simply by the media to which we are exposed. The first step toward taming the tongue is guarding our hearts and we can only do so successfully with God's help.

Day 2 – Focus

We began the process of taming our tongues with a prayer for God to help us guard our hearts. Next we need to gauge our tongue. A gauge is an indication used to tell how far you've gone or where your limits are. If our tongues had an actual gauge, there would be a place where we would stop.

Read Colossians 3:8. What is the instruction given?

____

____

It's definitely a challenge for some of us to stop letting anger, rage, slander, or bad language roll off our tongues. We have to determine we aren't going to say the things we used to say and we need God's help in this aspect of taming our tongues as well. We have to make the decision each day and manage it.

Write Psalm 141:3.

____

____

Repeat it daily as a prayer to God. Devise a plan to get ourselves under control when we face life's often enormous pressures.

Read Proverbs 10:19. What happens when words are many? Who is wise?

____

____

We can chose to be wise, by deciding not to cross certain lines with our tongues.

Day 3 – Foundation

Guarding our hearts and gauging our tongues is a great start for taming our tongues to speak life, but there is one more we need to add – garnishing our speech. When we think of garnish, we probably think of that little something we put on a plate to make it look prettier, more appetizing, after all 97 percent of food enjoyment comes from how it looks. What would it be like if we decided before we let any words roll off our tongues, we garnished them to make them sound pleasing to others?

____

Read Ephesians 4:29. What are we commanded to do (or not to do)?

____

____

Even in the times we need to say difficult words (correction, discipline, bad news), we can speak in a way to bless and encourage the other person. Bad news can be delivered in a positive way. Discipline can be delivered to benefit the one being corrected.

Write out Ephesians 4:31.

____

____

Sometimes the best thing to say is nothing at all. We see our perfect example Jesus hold His tongue many times. Sometimes, the lifegiving and life-preserving response is simply to keep quiet. Our soul will certainly protest but our spirit will gain strength as we take another step toward living God's way.

Day 4 - Reflect

Read the verses below and answer, "When is it a good idea to just say nothing?"

Proverbs 11:13 ____

Proverbs 13:3 ____

Proverbs 17:9 ____

Proverbs 17:14 ____

Proverbs 17:27-28 ____

Philippians 2:14-15 ____

The Lord wants to be near us, but we resist Him and His presence by some of the words we say. Sometimes we simply need to be quiet. Other times, we need to speak good words, build up others and ourselves, and in doing so, invite the presence of God into our lives so we can encounter Him in new ways.

Read the following and note the instruction on how to best use our tongues.

Proverbs 4:24 ____

Proverbs 15:1 ____

Proverbs 16:24 ____

Proverbs 16:28 ____

Ask God to shine the light on words you should never have spoken to others and words others should have never spoken to you. Move forward, speaking life.

Day 5 – Journal: Affirmations

As we close this week, let's read aloud theses declarations/affirmations and receive the truth from God's Word.

I am blessed with God's supernatural wisdom, and I have clear direction for my life.

I am blessed with creativity, with courage, with ability, and with abundance.

I am blessed with strong will, self-control, and self-discipline.

I am blessed with a great family, good friends, good health, and with faith, favor, and fulfillment.

I am blessed with success, supernatural strength, promotion, and divine protection.

I am blessed with an obedient heart and with a positive outlook on life.

I declare any curse ever spoken over me, any negative evil word that has ever come against me, is broken right now.

I am blessed in the city. I am blessed in the country. I am blessed when I go in. I am blessed when I come out.

Everything I put my hands to is going to prosper and succeed.

I am blessed!

Add more here:

Week 25: The Living Word – Change Your Life

Day 1 – Set the Stage

Read Joshua 1:7-8. What is commanded? What is promised if the commands are followed?

____

____

____

Imagine a friend offering to make you prosperous and successful in everything you do. He promises to give you the ability to rise above any circumstance and stand against any enemy. Following his direction will keep you from sin, destruction, and despair. These are God's promises to all who read His Word and apply His principles to their lives. Who wouldn't want this?

Are you regularly consuming the Word of God and letting its truth replace your old way of thinking? Why or Why not?

____

____

Read John 1:1-3. What does this tell you about the Word of God?

____

____

There is power in the Word of God to change your life. Jesus, present at the beginning, is the Word. Jesus and the Word of God are the same. The same power that is in Jesus is in the Word. The Word of God is powerful.

Day 2 – Focus

Jesus was manifested in the flesh as the Word, and we have the same words manifested on its written pages. If Jesus showed up in the flesh, would we have any trouble believing Jesus could heal anyone sitting there with us?

We have to receive that truth so the Word can work. The Word has not changed or lost its power; we've just stopped mixing it with faith. If you want to fall in love with Jesus, find Him in the Word, and make the Word a priority. If you want more power, consume more of His Word and the Word will come alive.

Read Isaiah 55:11. What does God Himself say about His Word?

The Word is Spirit and life. In order for us to understand the Word, we must study, but more importantly we must include the Spirit of God, otherwise the words will only be words on a page.

Read John 5:36-39. What is Jesus's warning?

Jesus was speaking to the Pharisees who knew the Scriptures better than anyone at the time – but Jesus pointed out there was more to knowing God than intellectually knowing the Scriptures. Why? The Bible can come alive and bring real change in your life. Are you reading the Bible out of duty or out of desire to know God?

Day 3 – Foundation

Read Luke 1:26-37. What stands out to you in this incredible story?

____

____

____

The Word is revealed when the angel Gabriel visits young Mary and tells her she is about to become mother to the Savior of the world. In this narrative, God's Word becomes life. Mary, not surprisingly, asks, "How can that be?" to which Gabriel responds, "Nothing is impossible with God."

The word "nothing" in Greek is two words: no *rhema*. *Rhema* is the Greek word for "word," meaning more specifically "revealed word." Have you ever experienced the *rhema* Word of God during a sermon or while reading the Bible – like the words spoke directly to your heart?

____

When the Word becomes revelation to you, no word God speaks will be void of the power for it to happen. Readjust your beliefs, views, and opinions to line up with the Word of God, and not the other way around. Look at Mary's testimony in Luke 1:38. What did she say?

____

After the Word became a revelation to her, she believed. She settled in her heart what God had spoken to her would be true. When the *rhema* Word came, she obeyed. Have you settled it in your heart that once you hear God speak, you will obey?

If the Word of God doesn't seem to be working for you, remember God is not looking for your understanding or even your cooperation; He is looking for your obedience. How, then, can we activate the Word of God in our lives?

First, we need to make God's Word a priority. Much like we need food as fuel for our bodies, our spirits need the Word. As we spend time reading the Bible, His Word will come alive to us. Read Romans 10:17. How often are you reading the Word?

Second, we need to meditate on the Scriptures. In other words, we need to read the Word, think about it, study it, repeat it, discuss it, journal it, and post it. Doing so paves the way for *rhema* or revelation to take place, and puts our faith into motion. Read Psalm 1:2. How often are you meditating on the Word?

Finally, we need to believe what we read, in other words, choose to believe the Word of God is true. God tells us it is impossible to please Him without faith. Faith makes prayer work. Faith comes from hearing the message, and the message is heard through the Word about Christ. Read Romans 10:17. Do you believe the Word is true?

God gives us revelation through His Word. The revelation gives us faith. Faith makes things happen!

Day 5 – Journal: Affirmations

As we close our week, let's take a few minutes to journal our thoughts and prayers based on what we have learned about God's Word. Include what God has taught you, what He wants you to do in response, or compose a simple prayer to Him. Here's an affirmation to get you started.

God wants me to be strong and courageous. He wants me to obey His instructions (His Word) and not deviate from them so that I will be successful in everything I do.

Week 26: The Living Word – Power in the Promises

Day 1 – Set the Stage

Read Joshua 1:8. What is the command?

____

____

What is promised as a result of obedience to the command?

____

____

Moses' successor, Joshua, had inherited the daunting task of leading the Israelites into the Promised Land. For his mission to be successful, he had to teach the Israelites some principles from the Word of God. The Israelites were instructed to study the Word, to meditate on it. If they did, God promised them prosperity and success in all they did.

Today, the word "meditate" has multiple connotations today, but the ancient Israelites understood exactly what they were being instructed to do here. The Hebrew word hagah translated "meditate" here means "to mutter, to ruminate." The first brings to mind a person muttering in obsession over his thoughts. The second "to ruminate" means to "chew the cud." In other words, get all the nutrients out and swallow it. Then, recall it again, chew on it some more, and swallow it again. Chew on it all day long, and you'll be able to do what it says. The Israelites understood "meditating" to be muttering and ruminating (chewing the cud) as the best practice for internalizing God's Word and the secret to having the Word come alive in their life. It is still true for us today!

Day 2 – Focus

What are some ways we can meditate on God's Word?

____

____

____

We already know one of the ways to mediate on God's Word is to read and study it daily, but that's not enough. We need to find Scripture we can speak. The purpose of speaking God's Word is not to convince God it's true but rather to remind us of its truth. When God's Word comes out of your mouth, it builds your faith. We can speak the Word over situations and circumstances in our lives, for example when we face challenges, trouble, or even spiritual battles.

Read 1 John 4:4 . Now, below, write the passage in first person and put your name in it.

____

____

____

____

How could speaking these Words help you in times of trouble?

____

____

When we speak His Word aloud over our lives, we are reminded of His love, His promises, and His power and we, as a result, recognize our power in Him to overcome!

Day 3 – Foundation

Study His Word. Speak His Word aloud over our lives. We now know these as
ways to meditate on His Word so we can live in obedience to Him and have both
the prosperity and success He desires for us. But there is another way – think
about His Word day and night. We can't simply be tuned into God for an hour of
our waking hours, with the rest of our time tuned into work, the media, or our
problems. Do you think that's the reason the "world" is more real to us than God
and His truth? Of course it is – we spend more time in the "world" than with God.
We need to bring our world and God's world together, and make them one. Our
secular world shouldn't be different from our sacred world.

In meditation, frequency is the key. It is not a matter of how much, but how
often. Reading the Bible three times a year may be a great goal, but it will be
meaningless if we aren't meditating on the Word. Consider starting one of these
practices today to help you truly meditate on His Word.

Read a verse 10 times in a day instead of reading through the Word for 30
minutes. Let's start with Proverbs 3:1-4. Read it through, underlining what we are
to do with God's Words. Make a plan to read it nine more times today.

Read a passage each day and note its benefits, promises, commands, lessons.
For example, read Deuteronomy 6:6-9 and list the actions we are to take in
regards to God's commands.

____

____

Day 4 – Reflect

Study His Word. Speak His Word aloud over our lives. Think about His Word day and night. We can already see the difference its making in our lives, can't we?

But there's one more thing – do what is written in His Word. Sometimes we are great at studying the Word, learning it, getting excited about it, but are we consistently doing what it says?

What would it be like if we truly started practicing the Bible?

Remember our promise in Joshua 1:8. If you want to be prosperous and successful, then here's the secret. "Meditate on it day and night so you may be sure to obey everything written in it. Only then will you prosper and succeed." The promises of God are fulfilled when we walk in obedience to His Word.

Read James 1:22-25. Look at verse 22, how do we deceive ourselves?

Now look at one of the spiritual laws of God in verses 23-25. What is the premise in this promise?

We need to make our Bible time sacred, no interruptions. We need to find our verse (S.O.A.P), say it aloud, think about it all day, do it, and watch what happens. Meditation will turn to revelation. Revelation will activate faith and things will change!

Day 5 – Journal – Affirmations

As we close this week, read the following verses and then write each passage in first person and put your name in it (the first one is done for you), speak these words over your life this week, do what is written, and watch God work!

Luke 10:19

God has given me (put your name here) power to tread on serpents and scorpions, and over all the power of the enemy: and nothing shall by any means hurt me.

Romans 8:37

Psalm 27:1

Philippians 4:19

Week 27: Perfect Love – True Authority

Day 1 - Set the Stage

We've made it to the halfway point in *A Year to a Better You*! Congratulations!

What positive changes have you seen so far?

What areas of concern or struggle do you still have?

Read Philippians 2:10-11. Who has all authority?

Jesus has all authority in heaven and on earth and under the earth. In order to realize our purpose and move toward our heavenly prize, we must be equipped in spiritual warfare and live each day as a worshiper of the One who is worthy of all glory and honor and power – Jesus.

Read Psalm 51:9-10. How do we get a firm foundation in spiritual warfare?

Our firm foundation in spiritual warfare is the extravagant love of God. As believers, we can be assured God is actively involved in our lives and provides safety in the shadow of His wings. If we continue to walk in fear, we have not yet comprehended the magnitude of the Father's love for us. God's Word tells us "perfect love casts out all fear" (1 John 4:18). The enemy continues to attack, but God has given us mighty weapons of warfare to demolish strongholds!

Day 2 – Focus

Read 2 Peter 1:3. We are equipped for success, by whom and for what?

____

____

____

A good starting point for overcoming the enemy is realizing we have been equipped to succeed in everything the Lord calls us to do by His mighty power.

In addition to having His calling on our lives, we actually get to choose the way and the degree to which we serve God. If we are not satisfied with where we are, there is always more. To be a vessel the Lord will use time and again, we must allow the Holy Spirit to examine our lives. When He shows us an area of sin, we must ask for forgiveness and turn away from it. The Lord doesn't condemn us; He convicts us so we can be our best and be the recipients of His best!

Read 2 Peter 1:5-11. What can we do to grow productive and useful in the Lord? What is our reward for doing so?

____

____

____

A victorious life begins and ends with worship and faithfulness. Faithfulness to Him and our worship toward Him helps us refocus from our personal circumstances and agendas to the Lord and His love, His provision, and His perspective.

Day 3 - Foundation

To have a solid foundation in His perfect love and come under His true authority, there are three things we need to know.

Read Acts 10:38. Who anointed Jesus? With what? What did Jesus do as a result?

____

____

____

In His full authority and with the power of the Holy Spirit, Jesus worked on behalf of those who were oppressed and attacked by the devil.

Read the following verses and note what each verse teaches us about demons.

Revelation 12:7-9

Demons are ____.

1 Peter 5:8-9

Demons want to ____.

Ephesians 6:10-12

Demons respond to a _______________________________________.

Demons are fallen angels. They seek to oppress, to destroy, and to devour believers. But most importantly, demons respond to the authority of God and a well-equipped believer.

Day 4 – Reflect

There are times when we are all afraid. Write about a time you were afraid and God gave you courage in the midst of your fear.

Now consider the following questions:

What place does spiritual warfare have in your life?

Why do we not need to be afraid?

How can we identify and defeat the enemy?

How did God display His grace, love, and friendship for us through the cross?

The benefits of the cross include payment for sin; healing from sickness and disease; the grace, love, and friendship of God; and eternal life with Christ. The enemy brings condemnation but the Holy Spirit convicts and forgives. We must equip ourselves – setting our mind on things above, taking every thought captive and making it obedient to Christ, putting on the whole armor of God. We have the victory in the full authority and perfect love of Christ.

Day 5 - Journal - Affirmations

Write 2 Corinthians 13:14 from the Message.

____

____

____

As we close our week, let's take a few minutes to thank the Lord for this promise as we affirm our lives in Him and enjoy the extravagant love of God, the amazing grace of Jesus, and the friendship of the Holy Spirit living in us.

____

____

____

____

____

____

____

____

____

Week 28: Perfect Love – Cast Out Fear
Day 1 – Set the Stage

We recently learned from 1 John 4:18, "Such love has no fear, because perfect love expels all fear. If we are afraid, it is for fear of punishment, and this shows that we have not fully experienced his perfect love." Let's learn more about the highest authority and why perfect love cast out fear.

Read Luke 10:17-19. What do you learn about who has the highest authority?

____

____

We know from this passage and others, God is the highest authority. As the Creator, God has authority over all of creation including man.

Read Genesis 1:26. What did God do? Who did he put in authority over the creatures of the earth?

____

God created man in His image and gave man authority over the rest of creation. Notice man didn't question God's authority to give authority but later Satan did (Genesis 3).

Read Isaiah 45:5-8. How does God describe Himself?

____

____

God is "the LORD, and there is no other." He created everything and as a result has authority over it all including mankind.

Day 2 – Focus

You may be wondering, what about Jesus's authority? Where does He fit in?

Read Matthew 4:1-11 and Luke 4:1-13. What do you learn about the authority of Jesus?

____

____

____

____

Authority proves doctrine (teachings). Authority has no validity unless it is based on truth. Doctrine is not truth without the proper authority.

Read John 1:1-4, 14. We know the Word is Jesus, so what more do you learn here about the Word?

____

____

The Word was God which means the Word had all the attributes of God including His authority – the highest authority. The Word spoke for God and as God. All things were created through Him. The Word became flesh and dwelt among us – clearly this indicates Jesus, so the Word was and is Jesus.

Read Matthew 28:18-20. What does Jesus declare?

____

Jesus had all authority before creation, during His time on earth, and He still has it – all authority in heaven and on earth for eternity.

Most of us have heard others declare, "God's Word is our authority." You may have even said it yourself. Why?

____

Read 2 Timothy 3:16. Who authored Scripture?

____

____

God's Word is indeed our authority because it was authored by God who is the ultimate authority. Every Word from God has the authority of God. The Bible's authority depends on the Author's power and sovereignty. The Word's authority is not dependent on us, whether we believe it or whether we obey it.

Each of us understands authority – we are exposed to it in various forms daily from stop signs to speed limit signs to traffic lights. In these instances, the authority comes from the government, and if we choose not to obey, we are subject to the consequences of our disobedience. The authorship of these laws is humanity.

The Bible's authority is supreme. Why? The Bible attests to its authority as the Word of God as we read in 2 Timothy. The Bible's fulfilled prophecies (more than 300 about Jesus alone) also attest to its authority. The Bible, while recorded by more than 40 writers has a single message, because the Words recorded are God's (2 Peter 1:20-21). Jesus also attest to the authority of the Word (John 17:17). But there is more, external evidence including the Dead Sea Scrolls and ongoing archaeological discoveries also confirm its authority.

Day 4 - Reflect

We know God's perfect love casts out all fear. We also know we can trust God and His Word because God is the creator and so the supreme authority over all. Even when we know these facts, fear can creep into our lives, a result of the devil's schemes. Here are three ways you can stand against the devil and allow God's perfect love to cast our all fears. Fill in the blanks as you read the following passages from the ultimate authority – God's Word.

James 4:7-8

Submit yourself to ____.

How?

____

2 Corinthians 2:10-11 and Ephesians 4:26-27

Close any ____.

How?

____

2 Corinthians 10:3-5

Confront your ____.

How?

____

Day 5 – Journal – Affirmations

As we close this week, let's take a few minutes to journal our affirmations, thoughts, and prayers. Record what God is teaching you and how He wants you to apply your newfound knowledge. Ask God for help in those areas where you are struggling.

Here's an affirmation to get you started.

When I submit to God, I can resist the devil and he will run from me.

Week 29: Being Vessels of Honor – A New Way of Living

Day 1 – Set the Stage

At this point most of us are learning a new way of living, as well as new ways of viewing God and ourselves. Note one new thing you've learned so far.

____

When we were still far away, He came looking for us with His overwhelming love. He forgave our sins, provides us an abundant life, and is even preparing a place for us in heaven. He also made us with specific skills and talents and a unique personality - attributes which can be used to reach others for Him and the new abundant way of life He wants for all.

Read 2 Timothy 2:20-21. How is Paul using analogy here?

____

____

Paul uses something familiar (household utensils) to describe our uniqueness as believers and how God uses us to fulfill our destinies. Some items are inexpensive and ordinary, but others are honorable, used for special occasions. In God's hands, every utensil can accomplish great things. Every one of us is at a different place in our walk with Christ. Our stories aren't the same. None of us started as gold or silver, but we are works in progress. God prepares us, refines us, and makes us honorable. Even if we don't feel honorable right now, God sees us this way. We are not defined or limited by our past. He makes all things new (2 Corinthians 5:17), and He wants each of us to be a vessel of honor. How do you want your life to be different?

Day 2 – Focus

Often we look at someone else's life and assume he or she is a stellar Christian. They may look holy and righteous, but appearances can be deceiving. We can't always tell from the outside what is going on inside their heart.

Read John 16:8. Are you willing to let the Lord examine your life and show you what is keeping you from being fit for every good work He has for you?

____

God wants to grow you to a higher level of personal integrity. He will do a miracle in your life if you let Him. Can you think of any areas the Lord needs to clean up in your life? Write them here and offer them to the Lord.

____

____

____

Earlier we learned justification is the moment Jesus becomes our Savior and every sin is wiped clean (Romans 8:33). We also learned about sanctification, which unlike justification is not an event, but the lifelong process of allowing God to make us more like Him. It is allowing Him to mold us and transform our character to make us vessels of honor for the Master's (His) service (2 Timothy 2:21). The Greek word translated as "master" is *dispotus*, meaning a ruler with absolute power and authority over others. Most often we think of God as Friend, Savior, Protector, which He is – but He is also LORD and Master. He is in charge and we become His servants before He can fulfill His purpose in us. (Yes, it means the servant level is the highest level.)

Day 3 – Foundation

In 2 Timothy 2:21, we read, "If you keep yourself pure, you will be a special utensil for honorable use. Your life will be clean, and you will be ready for the Master to use you for every good work." Why is keeping our bodies pure so significant?

Our bodies are the place sin functions (words from our mouths, what we view with our eyes, what we touch, etc.)

Read Job 31:1. What was Job's covenant? Why is it so important?

When we are intentional, our decisions are different and we are on our way to becoming a vessel of honor. Are you willing to say, "Here I am Lord, clean me up. Take each member of my body and the things I have done and wash me. Take my appetites, my addictions, my habits, my tongue, my attitudes, and consecrate them."

Write 2 Timothy 2:22. Underline or highlight the first word of each command.

Read Romans 6:12-14. Use it to guide your prayer offering your body to God.

There are four stages of Christianity - unbelievers become believers, believers become disciples and grow, disciples become leaders with a purpose, and leaders become servants. Circle where you are right now.

Read Matthew 20:26. Where do you want to be?

____

Read Romans 12:1-2. How can you get there?

____

____

____

We become servant-leaders when we act honorably, offering our bodies as living sacrifices and renewing our minds. Why renew your mind? If we are honest, we are living sacrifices that keep crawling off the altar. Sin functions in the body, but the mind controls the body. Sin begins in the mind.

Read 2 Corinthians 10:3-5. Why do we need to renew our minds?

____

____

Spiritual warfare is a part of following Christ and while as Christians, we all love God, many of us don't know how to fight. One of the ways we fight is by demolishing arguments, ideas, and thoughts contrary to God and His Word. We must take our thoughts captive and compare them to the truth of the Bible in order to win the war.

Day 5 – Journal – Affirmations

As we close this week, write down ways you can minimize your exposure to worldly thinking so you can better hear the voice of God. (Here's one to get you started.)

Cut back on television shows that aren't aligned with God.

____

____

____

____

Next, renew your mind by using Scripture to combat the lies of the enemy. Read these passages and note how you can take captive the lie of the enemy.

Lie of the Enemy: You are confused.

I Corinthians 2:16 ____

Lie of the Enemy: You are fearful.

2 Timothy 1:7 ____

Lie of the Enemy: There is no hope.

Jeremiah 29:11 ____

Lie of the Enemy: Something bad is going to happen.

Psalm 91:10 ____

Lie of the Enemy: God can't hear you.

Psalm 34:17 ____

Week 30: Being Vessels of Honor – Renew the Mind, Surrender the Will
Day 1 – Set the Stage

For many, the concept of renewing the mind is easier to comprehend than is the surrendering of the will.

Read Romans 12:2. Why is it important to surrender our will to His will?

____

____

Our bodies act out our sin. Our minds control our bodies – but our will controls our minds! As we surrender our will, His perfect will becomes the goal of our lives.

Jesus told us to pray, "Your kingdom come, Your will be done" (Matthew 6:10). He meant we should not come to prayer with an agenda. Instead we should approach Him with this in mind, "Lord, you are my Shepherd, I shall not want. What I want is what You want." We cannot manipulate God but must come to Him with a neutral heart. When we are leaning one way or another, God's voice is difficult to discern.

Read Luke 22:42. Jesus is praying in surrender to the Father's will, what can we learn from His example?

____

____

When we pray surrendering our will, we honor God with every part of our lives and we become vessels of honor, useful to the Lord. He then stirs up purpose within us so we can realize our dreams and reach others with the Good News about Jesus.

Day 2 – Focus

Read 1 Peter 2:9. Who are we as believers and what are we called to do?

____

____

Being useful members of God's kingdom comes with a price – we will get the attention of the enemy. We must anticipate his attacks and take them as a sign of encouragement; we are a threat to his plans to keep the world in darkness. The good news is we belong to God – the enemy cannot change that fact! We can also prepare for battle by studying the enemy's tactics. Our adversary knows he can stall our progress by trapping us in sin, often in the form of enticements (possessions, achievements, appealing circumstances).

Read James 1:14-15. What do you learn about temptation?

____

____

Temptation tests our character through our desires. Temptation leads to sin which leads to death.

Read James 1:13. From whom does temptation come?

____

God never tempts us! Satan and his demons are the tempters. As a created being, Satan cannot be everywhere at once but he and his servants are continually seeking to destroy our lives. Thankfully we can rest in the promise of 1 John 4:4, "He who is in us is greater than he who is in the world" so we can stand against temptation.

Day 3 – Foundation

Often, the enemy attacks us with ideas so subtle and tailormade for us we believe the thoughts are our own. The Bible says as believers we have the power within us to withstand every temptation of the enemy.

Read James 4:7. What happens when we resist the devil's temptations?

____

Read 1 Corinthians 10:13. What does God do when temptations seem unbearable?

____

Read Matthew 26:41. What advice does Jesus give to help us withstand temptation?

____

God always provides a way out in the midst of temptation. Jesus advises us to pray (keep communication with God open) during times of temptation so that we can remain safe and aware. We play an active role in our deliverance from evil – we can either succumb to the devil's temptation or we can submit to God and withstand the enemy by His power.

We know our enemy has already been defeated but we have to enforce his defeat in our own lives. A foothold gives Satan a base for advancing his destructive plans in our lives. Over time, as we give in to a particular temptation (sin), its control grows and the only way out is to confess the sin and repent.

Day 4 – Reflect

Often we believe admitting our sin clears our conscience and frees us from any consequences or responsibility. While admitting sin is part of repentance, it is not repentance. Repentance means to turn away from sin and choose not to continue in it.

Read 2 Corinthians 7:10. What might be missing in a person who struggles with turning from sin?

____

Read Romans 2:4. How does God help lead you to repentance?

____

If you are in a cycle of sin, don't give up hope! God wants to help you break the cycle.

Read Psalm 37:23-24. How can God help?

____

____

Ask Him to give you godly sorrow which leads to repentance. Meditate on His goodness and His kindness.

We were made to be vessels of honor, a status which includes fighting the enemy and reordering our lives. Though the battles can be messy, the rewards are immeasurable. God's Word promises obedience brings blessing (Deuteronomy 11:27). Allow God to use you as a catalyst for peace in your family, joy in your neighborhoods, and change in your schools and places of business.

Day 5 – Journal – Affirmations

As we close this week, pray as God leads you, whether you need a prayer of repentance, a prayer of submission/surrender to His will, a prayer to renounce areas in which Satan has a gained a foothold, a prayer for the Holy Spirit's guidance, or a prayer of thanksgiving for a victory He has given you.

Week 31: Worship is a Lifestyle – The Overflow of Relationship

Day 1 – Set the Stage

Hopefully, during the past months you realized God is completely in love with you. In response to His love, you have come to trust Him, and because of the relationship, you have fallen in love with Him. Being in love with God allows you to move from duty to devotion. Following His commands have turned from drudgery to desire.

An overflow of our relationship with God is worship. Worship is more than song; it is a lifestyle expressed through acts of service, words of affirmation, and gift giving, as well as singing, dancing, and even shouting. Living God's way produces purity, confidence, and strength in us and we become warriors in God's kingdom.

Read Isaiah 38:18-19. What does worship allow us to do?

____

____

____

Surprisingly, worship is an act of warfare against our enemy. In fact, our worship has the power to put the devil on the run and helps us fight against the power of darkness. As we offer praises to God, we strip the enemy of power over our bodies and souls. Through the blood of Jesus we can come boldly into the presence of God (Hebrews 4:14-16). Once and for all time, Jesus, our High Priest, "took his own blood, and with it He secured our salvation forever." (Hebrews 9:12). Salvation in Christ includes eternal life with God, healing for our souls, and deliverance from all the powers of the enemy. The very Presence of God now lives in our heart because of Jesus.

Day 2 – Focus

Read Revelation 12:10-12. Who is defeated here? Who is the victor?

      God declares Satan, the accuser of the believers who accuses them before God day and night, is overcome. The blood of Jesus has overcome Satan. As believers, we are fighting from victory – NOT to victory! The victory is already won; Satan is a defeated foe. Nothing is separating us from God's presence and as a result we can be in an intimate relationship with Him.

      Much like a bridegroom, He has declared His love for us; we simply need to receive His love and learn to love Him in return. Worship is the highest priority of the believer. The one thing God wants more than anything else is our hearts.

      Genuine worship comes directly from a heart connected with God. Our connection with God can happen in two ways: corporately (at church or other gatherings with fellow believers) and personally (anytime, anywhere). Corporate worship is crucial because our faith increases when we join in worship with like-minded believers. Even when we come to church or a small group distracted and burdened by cares, our attitude can quickly change in a worshipful environment. Personal worship is only accomplished when we take the initiative, adjust our attitudes, and cultivate an atmosphere of praise. Wherever we are, any time of day, we can have an attitude of worship and enjoy God's presence. How can you worship Him today?

Day 3 - Foundation

Though we each desire to have a real relationship with God – just like the one we've seen and heard is possible – sometimes it seems impossible, doesn't it? Have you ever tried to read the Bible only to find yourself reading the same verses over and over and making no progress at all? Have you prayed, but feel like your prayers are going unheard?

In times like these, when we feel this way, we may need to re-evaluate our level of surrender. God wants our trust as much as He wants our heart because without our trust, our heart can never be completely His.

Most of us have said, "You are Lord," but then there's a bump in the road, and we grab the steering wheel from Him. Most Christians get distracted attempting to find the happiest, most pleasurable, most successful way to live, when the very best way to discover God's will is to surrender our control. How? It begins when we admit, "My life is not my own. I've been bought with a high price, and I am Your slave by choice. What would you like me to do, King Jesus?"

When we surrender to His will, He leads us and blesses us abundantly. In His will, He grants us success, happiness, and pleasure.

Read Psalm 16:11. What is the promise?

Day 4 - Reflect

Today let's take a test. Don't worry, it's not that hard! There are four levels of control in worship, circle the one which represents where you are:

- Ankle-deep: We can enjoy refreshing in God's presence, but we remain in full command. We splash and play, then walk out of the river with no lasting effects on our lives.

- Knee-deep: The current of God (His Presence) can be felt, but we maintain control. We have a good view of those who've ventured into deeper waters, but we still find our security on the riverbank.

- Waist-deep: The stream of His presence is strong. We've walked into deeper water, fighting the current, and keeping contact with the bottom. Often the fear of what others will think or the fear of losing control will tempt us to go back to the riverbank. It is here we make a crucial decision: Who will be in control? God or me?

- The Middle of the River: Here we experience all of the river. We stop fighting for control, and, instead, pick up our feet and float, or allow His current to carry us. We go where He goes and it is good!

The vision of the river symbolizes the presence of God in our lives. The bottom and the bank represent the world. As we give up control to God, we begin to experience His Presence and live as He desires us to live. Most of us want to get wet, but still want to stay in control. In other words, we want to do the "God thing," but want to reserve just enough control so God doesn't take us too far. When we live this way, we have believed the lie that if we abandon ourselves to His control, He will make us do things we don't want to do.

Read Psalm 36:7-9. What is the truth?

____

God has only good things for His kids. We will never come to the place of true worship until we can honestly say, "God, have Your way."

Day 5 – Journal: Affirmations

As we close our week, let's journal where we are in our relationship with God and what is holding us back from going all in with Him. Ask God to help you reach the middle of the river, fully surrendered to Him. Here's an affirmation to get you started.

How precious is your unfailing love, O God! I find shelter in the shadow of your wings. You feed me from the abundance of your own house, letting me drink from your river of delights. You are the fountain of life, the light by which I see.

Week 32: Worship is a Lifestyle – Be a True Worshipper

Day 1 – Set the Stage

We know our relationship with Christ overflows to others in our lives and is also evidenced in our worship.

Read John 4:23-24. How then can we become true worshippers? What do true worshipers look like?

____

In John 4, Jesus said the time was coming when true worshippers would worship God in spirit and in truth. Read the following verses and then fill in the blanks.

2 Chronicles 16:9 – Give Him your __________________________________

God wants a covenant (devoted, unbreakable) relationship with us and it involves much more than singing songs. He wants us to desire and, more importantly, to enjoy His presence. We worship Him out of the overflow of our hearts because He is worthy of the best we can offer Him.

Daniel 3:17-18 – Remain _______________________________________.

The book of Daniel tells the story of Shadrach, Meshach, and Abednego and how they were to be thrown in a fiery furnace by King Nebuchadnezzar. Even so they remained committed to the LORD. We have to decide our level of commitment to God is unconditional. We aren't on this journey just because God is blessing us; we are in it because we are in a covenant relationship with Him. True worship means we praise God even when we don't feel like it; God is worthy of our worship in good times and bad.

Day 2 – Focus

Yesterday we learned if we want to be true worshippers we have to give God our hearts, our attention. We also discovered we have to be fully committed, worshipping Him unconditionally because He is always worthy of worship. Let's keep going, read the verse and then fill in the blank.

John 15:5 – Include Him in your _______________________________________.

We often struggle because our Sundays do not look like our Mondays. From the clothes we wear to the words we speak, we need to be consistent. When the "church world" becomes different than the rest of our world, it forces us to compartmentalize our lives. Our secular and sacred lives should look the same. What would happen if we made God a part of all our lives?

____

____

Often we struggle to make God fit into our lives – marriage, parenting, jobs, vacations, or hobbies but this is the ultimate sacrifice of worship. We need to include Him in our lives – 24 hours a day, seven days a week! Don't compartmentalize; He wants all of us because He loves us and cares what happens to us.

What area of your life do you need to include God? As we close today, write a prayer asking for guidance and committing to include God in this area of your life.

____

____

____

Day 3 - Foundation

Give Him our hearts. Remain committed. Include Him in our lives. God wants to be part of every part of our lives – it is how we truly become true worshippers. Let's continue and uncover the final actions we need to take to be true worshippers for life! Like before, read the verses and then fill in the blanks.

Genesis 22:14-18 – Be ____.

The first place in the Bible worship is mentioned is a story which reveals a heart of obedience and unconditional love for God. It is the story of Abraham laying Isaac on the altar. Abraham trusted God with the most important thing to him—his son—and this was called worship. Living according to what the Bible says is worship. Every day God invites us to join in His plans by prompting us to meet the needs of others, to stop and pray, or to enjoy time with our families, but often we ignore Him. Then Sunday rolls around and we "worship" Him and ask Him for things. Decide to be a worshipper who will focus your heart on worship every day. The greatest sacrifice we can give to God is a heart of humility willing to serve Him with unconditional obedience.

Proverbs 9:10 – Show ____.

Worship and fear of the Lord go hand in hand – in fact Jesus tells us they are the same, showing our reverence for the Lord (Matthew 4). The kind of fear He was talking about and the word "worship" are interchangeable, and Jesus, who is the Word, understood it perfectly. The Greek word for "worship" we read earlier this week in John 4:23-24 is *proskuneo* and it means "to kiss the master's hand in reverence." It indicates love and respect, along with the kind of fear that induces esteem and reverence.

Day 4 - Reflect

The word worship means we enjoy resting in His presence. Read the following verses and note what each says about fear, reverence, and worshiping the Lord.

Psalm 111:10 ____

____

Proverbs 1:7 ____

____

Proverbs 14:26 ____

____

Proverbs 14:27 ____

____

Proverbs 19:23 ____

____

Ecclesiastes 12:13-14 ____

____

Each day we have an opportunity to live and love well, in ways which line up with the Word of God. We can't separate our love for Him from our submission to Him. God says He wants us to not only worship Him in spirit with expression, gratitude, and intimacy, but also in truth. How, then, do we worship Him in spirit and in truth? We need to ask Him to purify us. Real worship is pure worship.

Day 5 – Journal: Affirmations

As we close our week, read this incredible promise aloud: "The person who has My commands and keeps them is the one who [really] loves Me. I will let Myself be clearly seen by him and make Myself real to him" (John 14:21, AMP).

We can't obey His commands and worship Him if we are falling short or have secret sin. God's desire is to purify us. If there is an area in your life you know you need to deal with, ask Him to forgive you.

Consider using this simple prayer or write one of your own below. Remember when God is our first love, He will do immeasurably more than we can ask or imagine (Ephesians 3:20). Choose to love Him with your whole life, and nothing will be impossible for you.

"Father, forgive me for offending you and for going my own way. I make no excuses for it; I confess my sin right now. (Say aloud anything you need to let go.) I want this sin out of my life, and I choose to turn away from it. I receive Your cleansing right now. I know You delight to show me mercy. Thank You, Lord, for letting me off the hook. Father, I make my decision to worship You in spirit and in truth. I worship You with all my heart and love You! In Jesus' Name I pray, Amen."

Week 33: Soul Care – Relational Formation

Day 1 – Set the Stage

Over these last months, we have learned much both individually and together. We know the depth and breadth of God's love for us. We know we can trust him. We have grown in our love for Him. We also know He desires to transform us fully, so we can experience the abundant life He desires for us.

Read 1 John 2:27. How does God accomplish this transformation within us?

____

____

____

He transforms us through soul care, spiritual formation via the Holy Spirit as the verse we just read describes. As believers, the Spirit of Christ lives in us. We are Christ's anointed, and His anointing teaches us the truth. With true spiritual formation, we are transformed, able to resist the lies of the enemy and his false teachers. Spiritual formation allows us to live deeply in the truths we receive from the Holy Spirit.

The central idea is we human beings were made for an interpersonal attachment and communion with God the Father by Jesus Christ through the indwelling of the Holy Spirit. Our relationship with God is an ontological (state of being, existence) reality for believers and the relationship is inherently transformational.

Read 2 Corinthians 3:17. What is the promise regarding our transformation?

____

____

Read the following verses and note what defines our relationship with God.

Galatians 5:16

____

____

Matthew 6:31-32

____

____

John 15:4

____

____

In these passages we see neither doctrine nor ethics can define our discipleship. We are instructed to remain in Christ in order to be nourished and thrive as believers, much like branches are nourished and strengthened by the vine. The relationship Jesus describes is part of following Him which provides transforming spirituality - our soul care. Genuine transformation, which is spiritual formation, in Christ comes through abiding, ongoing, personal intimacy with God the Father, through Jesus Christ the Son, by the Holy Spirit.

Have you experienced spiritual formation and if so how?

____

____

Day 3 - Foundation

The challenge to our spiritual formation is the original sin – the premise of all humans having inherited the consequences of the first sin in the garden of Eden – which leaves us disconnected from God at conception. Apart from God, mankind is morally weak and under the domination of sin's power. In the ethical sense, flesh denotes humans as mere man apart from the power of God and thus under sin.

Read Romans 13:14. How are we transformed (filled with the Spirit)?

____

____

____

To be filled with the Spirit means our spiritual capacities must be retrained by the Holy Spirit. It is challenging and often spiritual formation is slow. When we are dominated by our sinful nature, we think about sinful things. When we are controlled by the Holy Spirit, we think about things that please the Spirit. Letting our sinful nature control our minds leads to death. Letting the Spirit control our minds leads to life and peace. The sinful nature never obeys God's laws and is always hostile to God.

As believers we are not controlled by our sinful nature, but rather by the Spirit of God living in us. The Spirit of God, who raised Jesus from the dead, lives in us. We are instructed to put on the Lord Jesus Christ (clothing ourselves) and make no provision for the flesh (sin/evil desires) in regard to its lust. In this respect, all the unsaved live in the realm of the flesh (sin), fulfilling the desires of the flesh. Believers, on the other hand, are to get rid of the deeds of the flesh (sin), by the power of the Holy Spirit living within us.

Day 4 – Reflect

Getting rid of sin by the power of the Holy Spirit living in us is a task easier said than done. We are deeply habituated to live in autonomy from God and depend on ourselves. Sin is the obstacle to cultivating a deep dependence on God.

Read 1 Corinthians 3:1-4. Write 1 Corinthians 3:2.

____

____

What does Paul mean "you weren't ready for anything stronger"?

____

____

They weren't ready to receive the deeper spiritual truths and be truly transformed because of their sin nature. In modern terms, we might say they weren't ready because they continued to grab at what made them feel good or look more important. They were content when life was going well, the way they wanted it to go. Our flesh is in constant conflict with the spirit.

Write Galatians 5:17.

____

____

Paul tells us the desires of our flesh (sin nature) are contrary to the Spirit and the desires of the Spirit are against the flesh. In believers, the two are always battling, often keeping us from carrying out the good we want to do. We must let the Holy Spirit guide our lives, so we can avoid doing what our sinful nature craves.

Day 5 – Journal: Affirmations

As we close this week, write the following verses and note how we can put our sinful nature to death.

Colossians 3:5

____

____

Galatians 5:24

____

____

Romans 8:13

____

____

The Word tells us we can put our sinful nature to death, essentially crucifying the flesh. It sounds hard because it is. We can't put to death our sinful nature without the power of the Holy Spirit. What area do you need the Holy Spirit's power to help you overcome your sinful nature? Write a prayer asking God to help.

____

____

____

Week 34: Soul Care – Relational Transformation

Day 1 – Set the Stage

Last week, in Galatians 5:17, we read, "For the flesh desires what is contrary to the Spirit, and the Spirit what is contrary to the flesh. They are in conflict with each other, so that you are not to do whatever you want." As believers, many of us still struggle with our fleshly desires which tempt us to live independently from God. In our fleshly state, we are weak, yet God provides the strength we need to overcome our fleshly weakness by His Spirit.

We can all agree, the truth is, even as believers, we all still sin. So then, what is wrong?

____

____

It is quite evident the control of the Spirit does not happen for us automatically. We can't live the full life Christ has for us if we continue to obey our sinful nature (our flesh). As believers, we do have a choice – to follow our sinful nature or live by the Spirit and find true freedom.

The word Paul uses in Galatians translated as "flesh" is *sarx*, which means not only flesh (as in the body of a human or animal) but also the human (sensual) nature of humans apart from God. *Sarx* implies the dualistic nature of flesh and spirit. The flesh relies on human independence and accomplishments while the Spirit is founded in our dependence on God, which requires submission to His rule and plan. Are you living independently from God or in dependence on Him?

Day 2 – Focus

Living independently from God requires dependence on human values, systems, and customs to gain position, power, and allow for self-indulgence. In this form, independence is rebellion from the Spirit-filled life God wants for us. As the Word explains, trusting the flesh may seem to lead to the good life, but in reality it only leads to death. The flesh has multiple layers: relational ("walking according to the flesh"), internal ("desires of the flesh"), and behavioral ("deeds of the flesh"). The relational layer is based in our desire to be god rather than trust God. The internal layer is found in our longing to fulfill ourselves apart from God. The fact that we all sin in thoughts, words, and actions is relational. As we desire to fill ourselves apart from God, we sin in our words and deeds.

Why is it so hard to live in dependence on God?

____

____

A lot of the issue is habit. When we come to God, we bring our idols with us. Death is required to bring new life and our idols have been our defense and our resistance. How do we overcome the problem?

____

____

We can be receptive to the Spirit's presence. We can give up (die to) our attempts to find meaning apart from the Spirit. The discipline of confession and repentance, that is acknowledging the ways we idolatrously resist the spirit, is crucial.

Read Ezekiel 36:26-27. What promises does God make?

____

____

God promises a new heart and a new spirit to believers. God's Spirit allows us to live God's way according to God's will. As believers, we have the power to live a Spirit-filled life, in obedience to God, and receive His favor and blessing.

Read Jeremiah 31:31. What is the promise?

____

____

Read John 14:16-17. What is promised?

____

____

These verses confirm Ezekiel's prophecy which fulfilled the new covenant, ushered in with Jesus death and resurrection. As believers in Jesus, God's Word is written in our hearts as His people and the Holy Spirit lives within us and guides us in all truth.

You are a beloved child of God and God is a being with unlimited intelligence, power, and goodness who knows what you need and has committed to love and care for you forever. How does knowing this lead you toward the relational transformation available in Him?

____

As we reflect on the relational transformation available to us, let's read the following verses and answer, "What do you learn about the relational transformation which comes through life in Christ and soul care?"

Philippians 4:11-13

____

____

2 Timothy 4:16-17

____

____

2 Corinthians 12:9-10

____

____

2 Timothy 2:1

____

____

True relational transformation comes when God becomes the One we trust to keep us, when we abide in Him understanding we don't have to work to enjoy His salvation. When we are truly transformed, we consent to total dependence on Him, allowing Him to do everything in us, for us, and through us all we have to do is trust Him and allow Him to do it!

Day 5 – Journal – Affirmations

As we end our week of study, what areas do you see the need for spiritual formation in your life in order to experience the good life the Lord wants for you?

____

____

____

____

Journal your thoughts and prayers based on your answer. Include what God has taught you and what He wants you to do going forward. Here's an affirmation to get you started.

_______ *Jesus promised if I remain in Him, He will remain in me. He also said, in order to bear*

fruit I must remain in Him. ____

____

____

____

____

____

____

Week 35: Dark Night - Consolation
Day 1 - Set the Stage

We've learned so much about our freedom in Christ since we began. We have witnessed and experienced His great love for us in many ways. Through it all, we have learned to trust Him as we have grown more in love with Him. We have discovered the ways soul care and spiritual formation allow us to abide in Him, to experience the abundant life He has for us.

As believers, we also know living the life of a Christ follower also means challenges and dark times. Read 1 John 2:12-14. What phrase does John repeat to remind us that in spite of dark times we can overcome?

____

____

____

We have the ability to overcome because Christ lives in us and as a result we are strong and can overcome the evil one and the dark times which come into our lives.

This week, we are going to learn more about the stages and seasons of spiritual development and how God uses even the dark times in our lives for His divine purposes – to help us mature in Christ and love Him more. As we study what is referred to as the "dark night of the soul" we will learn about the purpose of consolation and desolation. The topic is challenging but we will soon discover consolation and desolation are less about actions and more about God's gifts to us in order to achieve His purpose in our lives.

The first state of spiritual development is, not surprisingly, the "beginner." It is the point in which we, as believers, understand we are God's children and we love God. We realize our sins are forgiven and we know the Father. It is a period characterized by spiritual pleasure. As a mother provides milk to her children, God feeds us the "bottle of spiritual pleasure" without any labor on our part during this stage. We experience a new affection at our core in which The Holy Spirit dwells. Often, those around us cannot see the change in us at the beginning except as it is manifested in our excitement. Our souls are moved due to the "consolation" of pleasure we get from "spiritual things" sought for their pleasure and not for God's glory alone. It is here that our spiritual strength begins to grow.

Stage 2 is known as "sins of the beginner." Our spiritual "change" deludes us into believing our energy and fortitude brought the consolation of God while our desires remain similar to our pre-converted days. Though we are indwelt by the Holy Spirit, much of our character is still filled with the flesh. The main difference – the Spirit is giving pleasure without which we would likely not go on and we have a new affection at our core. We hope to fulfill our appetite for pleasure and also feel good in our newfound spirituality.

Stage 3 is known as the "dark night" – the times in which God is growing us to love Him for His sake. We find our true selves and our hidden heart revealed here. We aren't alone – all the heroes of our faith faced the dark night of the soul in their lives. What stage are you in right now?

____

Day 3 – Foundation

The "dark night" is the time of desolation. What is happening when we experience these times?

____

____

We all experience desolation, most often at times when our character is more mature than it was in the beginning stages of our relationship with Christ. How, then should we understand these times in light of New Covenant Truths?

____

____

Read Colossians 1:27 and 2 Peter 1:4. What are the promises here?

____

____

How can these promises help us overcome when dark times come into our lives?

____

____

As believers, no matter what we are facing we have the promise of Christ in us – our hope of glory! We are also promised the power of His might, as well as all the blessings He has promised, in particular those to save us when the evil surrounds us even in the darkest of times.

How can we know God's promises to us are true in our deepest times of darkness and desolation?

____

____

____

Read 1 Corinthians 6:17 and then Romans 8:35, 37-39. How can we know God's promises to us are true in our deepest times of darkness and desolation?

____

____

____

____

____

Did your answer change? Why or why not?

____

____

____

God is always with us. He will never leave us or forsake us. He is everywhere. Though we know He never leaves us, many of us have felt what seems like God's absence in our lives. Yet for those who know Him best, we know God may actually be more present when we feel His absence than when we feel His presence.

Day 5 – Journal: Affirmations

As we close out this week, write out Psalm 23:4 and Psalm 34:18 as affirmations of God's presence even in the midst of the "dark nights of the soul."

Consider penning a prayer to God asking that He bring His promises to mind when you are in the dark times of desolation.

Week 36: Dark Night - Desolation
Day 1 - Set the Stage

As we continue to study the "dark night" and the concepts of consolation and desolation, what do you believe is the purpose of consolation?

____

____

____

The purpose of consolation is to give believers a taste of the presence of God even before our character development has begun to direct our hearts toward Him. Character development comes when we pray, read and study the Word, fellowship with other believers, join in service to the Lord, and more.

Read Psalm 34:8 and Psalm 119:103. How do these describe our consolation and subsequent character development?

____

____

____

____

____

As we experience consolation, we are able to give ourselves over to the spiritual disciplines of the Word, prayer, fellowship, service, etc. as God's love reinforces these behaviors.

Day 2 – Focus

What is the purpose of desolation?

____

____

When we experience desolation, we reveal what is truly in our hearts. It is in these times we see ourselves as we truly are: the hidden parts of our hearts which have yet to be yielded to God, the places we continue to cling to our idols, and the areas where we want to be god ourselves. The desolation – the dark nights of the soul – are significant and meaningful marking the point our lives in which God believes we are ready to see the truth about ourselves. He withdraws consolation so we can see our need clearly and make us hungry for Him.

Read Deuteronomy 8:2-3. Describe the "dark night" the Israelites experienced.

____

____

They wandered 40 years in the wilderness waiting to enter the Land of Promise. Their limits were pushed. They were tested. They faced hardships and hunger. They were disciplined. They learned much and grew in their relationship with God. God answered prayers and provided so they would understand their need to obey His commandments and follow Him wholeheartedly. They experienced His outrageous love.

Desolation is a gift in which we experience the truth of ourselves but more importantly we become hungry for God in new ways.

Read Psalm 42. Have you experienced this kind of longing for God? If so, when? What was the final outcome?

____

____

____

____

God does not withdraw from us during the dark night of the soul, but He does withdraw the feeling of consolation. God draws near to us to speak truth to us. His desire is to take us to new places of need and dependence on Him. During this time, our vices, which are often hidden, are on display. God can handle us, but we often cannot handle ourselves. In times of desolation, our true character is revealed because our will is at a great low.

When we are in the dark night, it is difficult to stay focused on or perform our spiritual disciplines. Spiritual things cause us to feel anxious and nervous, we wonder if we are backsliding, we think a new environment will make us feel better, everything feels different, and we believe the issues are everyone else's. Temptations are increased, we feel guilty, we work harder to get back to the way we used to feel, we worry, we are in despair often asking, "God, what are you doing?"

When we are experience the "dark night" (some of us may be even now), cry out to God, "Open my eyes to see what you are doing, what you are showing me, and how I can cooperate." God is always with us and He will answer!

Day 4 – Reflect

Let's reflect today on what we should do during the "dark night" as well as what we should not do. Write your thoughts here.

____

____

First, don't become silent, instead keep talking to God. Tell Him exactly how you feel and lament. If you are at a loss for words, seek out Scripture for guidance.

Read Psalm 39. What role do our spiritual disciplines play during this time?

____

____

During our time of desolation, spiritual disciplines have a completely different purpose. Rather than encouragement, during the "dark night" spiritual disciplines act as a mirror. We have to let ourselves be open to the mirror, letting it enter and magnify our lives. We must deal with the temptation to fix ourselves. Why? The point of the "dark night" is to show us we cannot fix ourselves, only God can. We have to avoid the temptation to generate consolation.

The answer is not to pray harder or longer but to tell God how you feel. We have to discover what the Holy Spirit is doing in us. We have to take our journey, being faithful to continue in the spiritual disciplines. It is crucial that we allow the Lord to meet us in those places. During the "dark night," God's Holy Spirit is inviting us into love, but it requires a journey through our hidden heart. During our journey, we sink into the truth of ourselves with Holy Spirit and God's love meets us in those places.

Day 5 – Journal – Affirmations

As we close our week, it is crucial to understand that going through the "dark night" is challenging, but on the other side, we find we've grown and experienced God's outrageous love for us in ways we could never have imagined. Journal your affirmations, thoughts, and prayers, based on what we have learned over the last two weeks. Include what God has taught you and what He wants you to remember when you face the "dark night."

Week 37: Staying Free – The Commitment

Day 1 – Set the Stage

We have studied our freedom in Christ and now have a deeper understanding of the great gift it is - allowing us to live the abundant life God has for us. This week, let's make the commitment to stay free.

Read Ephesians 1:19-20. What is the promise here?

____

____

In this fallen world, we face the harsh reality of many dark things: abuse (sexual, physical, emotional, verbal, and spiritual), violence, and betrayal. All create deep, serious wounds, but healing is possible; freedom is possible, and it is for each of us because God is good and gracious. His heart's desire is that we are completely whole, alive, and new in every way. He wants to see restoration happen for us even more than we do!

The path we are on - the one which led us to freedom in Him is part of our healing. The season we are in is part of the greater work the Lord wants to do in our lives. In our commitment to our study, *A Year to a Better You*, we have grown closer to the One Who's Name is Healer and He has promised to bring each of us to a new place of healing, restoration, and ever-increasing freedom.

All we need do to begin our commitment to stay free is go after God wholeheartedly in all we do. The Lord promises freedom, healing from the deepest wounds, and full restoration.

Day 2 – Focus

As we commit to stay free, we have to understand God heals our wounds and sets us free in a number of ways. Among us, we may have those who were healed and set free by Christian counseling, fellowship with a Biblical community, prayer, and time with Him. The Lord works healing and miracles in these ways and more. On our journey to stay free we have to keep pressing into the Father, allowing Him to show us the path He has for us.

There are no instant results, no immediate transformations, but through a trust-filled relationship with Jesus we can experience complete healing, restoration, and freedom for a lifetime and into eternity. A relationship with Jesus is completely authentic and permanent, but often the enemy attacks making us doubt our healing and our freedom.

When we face Satan's attacks it is crucial we clothe ourselves in the armor of God and allow Him to strengthen us to stay on the path to everlasting freedom. If the challenge seems to difficult, reach out for counseling or support from trusted friends and brothers and sisters in Christ. The enemy wants us doubting ourselves and God, and filled with shame and anxiety about the past from which we have been cleansed.

Read Jeremiah 29:11. What is God's promise to believers?

____

____

We must choose to believe what Jesus says about us not lies of the enemy. The Holy Spirit will always help us to remain free when we make the commitment to do so.

Day 3 – Foundation

We have a choice in regard to how we live today. Will you allow yesterday to dictate today, or will you turn, look at yesterday, and commit to remain free?

Ask the Lord to help you – He wants you to be free so much so He was willing to die so you could be free. The cross doesn't minimize our circumstances, but it always changes the outcome because it represents the power that conquered every sin and even death.

Read Philippians 3:13-14. Where does Paul keep His focus? How can doing so help us remain free?

We've come a long way so far, we are still the same individuals but also completely new – having tasted true freedom in Christ. We think, see, and do things differently than when we started this study. We're not as concerned about what's behind, but are looking ahead to all that is better – all God wants for us! We are looking at a future of freedom, filled with hope. This freedom is indeed an incredible thing, but it is only the beginning. Staying free requires a daily commitment – one for which God has fully equipped us!

What can we do when we find ourselves under attack from the enemy, making us doubt our freedom and wonder at our former issues?

____

____

____

As mentioned, as believers, we are equipped to face any attack. Our freedom is even more important to God than to us. Read the following verses and note how important your freedom is to God.

Galatians 5:1

____

2 Corinthians 3:17

____

John 8:32

____

John 8:36

____

Romans 8:1-4

____

You have the tools to remain free on your journey, so press on, and discover all the incredible things God has in store for you.

Day 5 – Journal: Affirmations

As we close our week, let's take a few minutes to journal our affirmations, thoughts, and prayers, based on what we have learned. Here's an affirmation to get you started.

It is for freedom Christ set me free; as one who knows the Son, I am free indeed.

Week 38: Staying Free – The Prize
Day 1 – Set the Stage

Staying free is founded in the truth Paul wrote to the Church at Philippi in Philippians 3:13-14, "But I focus on this one thing forgetting the past and looking forward to what lies ahead, I press on to reach the end of the race and receive the heavenly prize for which God, through Christ Jesus, is calling us." Staying free means focusing on the prize, but just how do we do so practically in the 21st century?

____

____

This week we'll take a slightly different approach as we discover how we can focus on the prize and remain free.

Read Psalm 119:105. What is the first step to focus on the prize and stay free?

____

____

We have to live by the Word, choosing to rearrange our thinking to line up with the Word of God, rather than trying to force Scripture to line up with our thinking.

Read Ephesians 6:11. What is step two in our quest to focus on the prize and stay free?

____

____

We have to put on the whole armor of God. A great way to start is by memorizing Ephesians 6:10-18 and putting on our protective armor daily.

Day 2 – Focus

Live by the Word. Put on the whole armor of God. Now onto the next steps in our journey to focus on the prize and stay free. Read the following verses and record the next steps in our quest.

Psalm 150:6

We must be true worshippers, allowing the power of worship to keep us pure. As we already learned, worship is also a powerful weapon to wield against the enemy.

2 Corinthians 5:7

We need to walk by faith, deciding to trust God and His Word, even when, in the natural world, it seems unlikely.

1 Thessalonians 5:17

We must maintain a daily prayer life, always talking to God and listening for His answers.

Ephesians 4:22-24

We have to change our old habits. When God shows us something in our lives which is holding us back from His best for us, we must make the decision to give it to Him.

Day 3 – Foundation

Live by the Word, put on the whole armor of God, be true worshippers, walk by faith, pray daily, and change our old habits to keep our focus on the prize and remain free. Read the following verses and record the next steps in our journey.

Romans 13:1

We have to submit not only to the Lord but to those who are in authority. Obedience is what we do with our bodies; submission is how we feel with our hearts. God wants submission, not just obedience.

James 5:16

We need an accountability partner – at least one person who knows all our secrets and still loves us, is committed to praying for us regularly, and will constantly reflect Jesus to us.

2 Corinthians 6:14

We must develop right relationships with our spouse, closest friends, and mentors, as well as those who are lost.

Joshua 7:13

Clean our house, asking God to show us anything which doesn't reflect Christ.

Day 4 - Reflect

Live by the Word, put on the whole armor of God, be true worshippers, walk by faith, pray daily, change our old habits, submit to authority, have an accountability partner, develop right relationships, and clean our house. Read the following verses and record the last steps needed to keep our focus on the prize and remain free.

James 4:7

____

Resist the enemy by being alert to his schemes and closing all open doors.

2 Timothy 4:18

____

Last, we need to always remain kingdom-focused, remembering we are ambassadors of heaven sent to reproduce heaven here on earth.

We know, "It is for freedom that Christ has set us free. Stand firm, then, and do not let yourselves be burdened again by a yoke of slavery" (Galatians 5:1). Let's rewrite the 12 steps which can help us focus on the prize and remain free.

____

____

____

____

____

Day 5 – Journal: Affirmations

Instead of our usual journaling and affirmations this week, use this prayer as an outline to help you prepare to stay free each day. First, put on the Armor of God, and then ask the Holy Spirit to give you wisdom, guide your steps, and help you stand firm to fight against the enemy.

Thank you, Lord, for my salvation (helmet). I receive it in a new and fresh way from you and I declare nothing can separate me now from the love of Christ and the place I shall always have in your kingdom. And yes, Lord, I wear your righteousness (breastplate) today against all condemnation and corruption. Fit me with you holiness and purity—defend me from all assaults against my heart. Lord, I put on the belt of truth. I choose a lifestyle of honesty and integrity. Show me the truths I so desperately need today. Expose the lies of which I am unaware. I choose to live for the gospel (shoes) every moment. Show me where you are working and lead me to it. Do not let me be slack in my walk. Jesus, I lift the confidence that you are good against every lie and every assault of the enemy (shield). You always have good in store for me. Nothing is coming today to overcome me because you are with me. Holy Spirit (sword), show me specifically the truths of the Word of God I will need as I counter the snares of the enemy. Bring them to mind throughout the day. With this in mind, be alert and always keep on praying for all the saints. Holy Spirit, I agree to walk in step with You in everything—in all prayer as my spirit communes with you throughout the day.

Identity

Week 39: More than Meets the Eye – The "I" in Lie

Day 1 – Set the Stage

We've all heard about the Titanic - the finest vessel of its day - larger, faster, and better equipped, boasting state-of-the-art engineering and shipbuilding. It afforded wealthy travelers every luxury. Deemed "unsinkable," those onboard felt protected, pampered, and privileged. If ever a ship seemed destined for success, it was the Titanic, everyone believed the ship could withstand any challenge. An employee of the White Star Line even declared, "Not even God himself could sink this ship."

Then the unthinkable happened - at 11:40 p.m. on Sunday, April 14, 1912, five days into her maiden voyage, the Titanic's lookout sent an urgent message to the bridge, "Iceberg, right, ahead." In less than forty seconds, the ship hit the iceberg. Within three hours, the Titanic was resting on the bottom of the Atlantic Ocean. More than 1,500 lives were lost.

Much like the Titanic, many people possess all the trappings of success, decked out with all that the world finds impressive - good looks, designer clothes, the best car, the right address, a sterling educational pedigree, a broad professional network, strong skills, and a bright mind. They seem destined to succeed but sometimes they crash and burn without explanation. The world places a high value on who we are outside, paying little attention to who we are inside.

Read 1 Samuel 16:7. How does the world's viewpoint differ from God's?

Day 2 - Focus

The difference between success and failure is not in the degree we obtain, the position we hold, the label we wear, the car we drive, or the amount of money we have obtained. The difference is what is on the inside, who we really are at our core, beneath the trappings of success. It's our internal dynamics which cause us to sail or sink in life. While relationships with others are important, our relationship with ourselves is vital.

One of the stories that best illustrates my point regarding identity and the relationship with self is the downfall of former NBC News Anchor, journalist Brian Williams. In 2007, he was one of Time Magazine's Most Influential People. In 1996, he was the National Father of the Year. He won twelve Emmys, appeared on Sesame Street, Saturday Night Live, the Olympics, and Late Night with Jimmy Fallon, just to name a few. In 2014, his salary was $10M per year. In 2015, at the pinnacle of his success, he lost his influence and credibility and was suspended from his job without pay. The respect he had gained was his to lose and lose it he did. There was no scandal, nor journalistic error. He lost it because he wanted more - more acclaim, more oohs and aahs, a chance to show more bravado on the television screen - and so he lied. He claimed to have been riding in a helicopter in 2003 in Iraq which came under heavy fire and was hit. The crewmembers on board called his bluff. People in America and around the globe were stunned, asking, "Why would he do this to himself?"

Read 1Timothy 6:9-10 and James 4:6. What might the be reason?

____

____

____

Day 3 - Foundation

Often when we orchestrate our own demise or our own delays on the road to success, we try to explain it away. Sometimes those explanations fall short because our insights into our own souls are not as clear as they should be. They are dulled, clouded by our desire to view ourselves in the most positive ways, rather than the most honest ways. These personal struggles come because we fail to understand our true identity.

We've all heard stories like Brian Williams' tragic fall. Why do they happen?

____

____

We tend to assess/esteem others on their external qualities - tangible assets, such as educational credentials, physical attractiveness, financial strength (or apparent financial strength, which may be nothing more than debt), professional experience, social position, or worldly influence, and assume they are successful. We also factor in intangible qualities – personality, charisma, and intelligence.

We take the same approach toward ourselves. When we struggle, we immediately try to fix something external to feel better about ourselves. Sooner or later, we realize that while they may have provided temporary relief they did not solve our problem – we're still wrestling with the same challenges. While external factors contribute to success they don't form the bedrock for a successful life.

Read Proverbs 23:4 and Matthew 6:33. What leads to genuine success?

____

____

Day 4 - Reflect

While outward accomplishments can move us forward, they will never bring us true, lasting success. In order to experience and attain genuine success, we have to understand our true identity which affects our relationships with others, but it is also the basis of everything especially our relationship with ourselves. It's unrelated to what we have working for us on the outside but all about what's happening on the inside - our thoughts, emotions, motives, and self-talk. In fact, it's foundational to how we relate to ourselves. It is self-esteem, self-respect, and integrity - the "why" behind what we think, say, and do. It's the combination of internal dynamics which forms us, shapes our character, and influences our life far more than we realize.

Think again about Brian Williams. His lie about being in the helicopter wasn't the real problem. The real issue was what was going on inside him to make him tell the lie - something on the inside made him feel deficient. Why did he feel he was deficient, given how good he already was? Why do we feel deficient even when things are going well?

Williams felt he was still lacking, not good enough. The acclaim and fame and fortune he had were not enough to empower him to see himself as others saw him. The world saw him as nearly perfect, but he didn't see himself that way and felt he had to make himself look better. The same is true for us, we always feel the need to make ourselves look better.

Read Ephesians 1:11-14. Where do we gain true worth?

Day 5 – Journal – Affirmations

As we close this week, let's pray asking God to show us areas in which we feel we need to lie to feel better about ourselves.

____

____

____

____

____

Next, write promises or affirmations from God's Word regarding your true worth.

Here's an affirmation to get you started.

_____ _God gave me worth when He purchased me to one of His own people._ _____

____

____

____

____

____

____

____

Week 40: More than Meets the Eye – You are the Key to Your Success

Day 1 – Set the Stage

Often, when we fail to reach our goals, fall short of achieving our destiny, or tumble from our place of position or prominence, we dive right into the "blame game." Almost immediately, we find a reason things did not work out as we hoped. Typically it goes like this: "That opportunity didn't work out for me because that company never hires people from my alma mater" or "I didn't get the job because of my gender" or "I ended up with an addiction because I needed to numb the pain of my past" or "my marriage fell apart because my parents divorced and never taught me the relational skills I needed." We get the idea, having heard people blame their problems and shortcomings on everything from their parents to their children to the government to their race, age, or gender, or to the neighborhood in which they grew up.

When disappointments or troubles happen to us as Christians, we often blame the enemy, making comments such as: "The devil is trying to steal my destiny" or "I'm under attack from the enemy! He's hindering my success!" While I am quick to affirm the reality of spiritual warfare, the hard truth is more often than not, no person, no organization, and no situation is responsible for what happens in our lives. Almost always, it is something within us as individuals that causes our greatest frustrations. Many times, we are our own worst enemies. Can you remember a time when you were your own worst enemy?

____

____

Day 2 - Focus

Rather than being our own worst enemies we can be our own advocates and best friends. Let's compare those who sabotage themselves to those who position themselves for success. People who sabotage themselves allow their ego to get in the way, while those who position themselves for success are secure in who they are, yet humble. Those who sabotage themselves nearly always refuse advice and turn down help. Those poised for success seek good advice and implement it.

When we criticize ourselves, are unable to manage our anger, greed, jealousy, lust, or other emotions, we sabotage ourselves. On the other hand, when we accept ourselves and control our anger and other negative emotions we set ourselves up for success. We often sabotage ourselves when we fear failure and lack self-confidence. When we seek to learn from our failures, we grow in self-esteem, character, and abilities.

Read 1 Samuel 1-4. What do you learn about Hophni and Phinehas?

____

____

Hophni and Phinehas were the sons of Eli, a priest in Israel. They were also priests. They served the Lord externally but not internally, not in their hearts. They were not in fellowship with the Lord. No matter what they did or who they were with, they brought no value to the situation. Has there been a time in your life when you have fallen out of fellowship with the Lord and your success was effected?

____

Day 3 – Foundation

Yesterday we met Hophni and Phinehas. To the worshippers in the temple, they may have seemed successful in their responsibilities of serving the Lord, but they clearly had many private failures (greed, sexual sin, etc.) which undermined their public success. Ultimately, they were killed in a battle with the Philistines in which the Ark of God was captured. On hearing the news, Eli their father and Phinehas' wife also died. In the case of the two brothers, Israel was at war with its enemy, the Philistines. At one point in the battle, the Israelites were asking, "Why? Why are we being defeated?"

They did not recognize their greatest weakness – God was not with them. Even worse, they did not realize the reason He was not with them – because of the true identity of their priests, Hophni and Phinehas. The Israelites thought regaining the Ark of the Covenant would guarantee their victory. It wouldn't – because doing the right things externally is never sufficient. In fact, the Israelites were defeated long before the battle even started because their leaders never addressed their real relationship with God.

The ability to succeed or not resides within us. It's true, there are times when others can help us succeed, or circumstances fall into place perfectly. Yes, there are times God moves on our behalf in astonishing ways to help us. Success rises and falls on each individual but sadly, we are often the greatest hindrance to our success and the greatest barrier to all God wants to do in and through our lives.

Read Proverbs 14:12. How do we get in God's way and become a barrier?

Going our own way without God is never the way to the success He wants for us.

Day 4 – Reflect

In many ways, life is a battle. We wrestle with financial issues, relational issues, bad habits and addictions, poor choices, trying to get ahead personally or professionally, and other challenges that everyday life presents. In order to succeed we have to fight. We have to fight external enemies, but we also have to fight the internal forces that cause us to sabotage ourselves. In order to win the battles necessary to succeed in life, we have to:

- Realize not every hindrance, delay, or challenge we face is external. In fact, some of the most potent are internal.

- Deal with the weaknesses and negative aspects of ourselves. It is not a quick-and-easy process, but the rewards are tremendous.

- Replace the faulty elements of ourselves with strong, healthy ingredients. In doing so, we turn the things which hinder us into things that help us.

We are destined for so much more than we are currently experiencing. Our lives can be so much better than they are now, better than we have ever imagined. We have many gifts, skills, talents, and dreams just waiting to take us to the next level. Our externals may be in order but we have to work on our internals.

How would you describe your relationship with yourself? What areas need to change to get you to the next level of success God has for you?

____

____

____

Day 5 - Journal - Affirmations

True success is not dependent on external resources or evident in the so-called external trappings of success. It comes from what's inside you. As we close our week, let's take a few minutes to journal what we've learned this week about our relationship with ourselves and with God as well as how we can get out of God's way and find our true success in Him.

____

____

____

____

____

____

____

____

____

____

____

Week 41: It's Time to Peel the Onion – Your Identity is NOT Based on Your Circumstances or What You Do

Day 1 – Set the Stage

The issue of personal identity is a huge component of our success. Everything we think, everything we do, and the entire way we see and relate to ourselves flows from our sense of identity—our personal assessment of who we are and why we are significant. Our identity is the compass guiding us through every aspect of our lives, keeping us grounded and centered in the things which matter most. When we are not secure in our identities, we waste so much time in our efforts to fulfill unreasonable expectations others have placed on us.

Many of us have crashed and burned not because of our own inabilities or weaknesses, but because we tried to be someone else in an effort to please people who never should have had so much influence on us in the first place. Trying to please or impress other people, or to live up to their expectations, is exhausting and frustrating. We rarely succeed trying to please others because all the while we are suppressing and denying our true selves, pretending to be someone we are not!

We need to know our true value because when we do we are so much more authentic and can enjoy the life God wants for us.

Read John 3:16. How did God show us just how valuable we are to Him?

____

____

____

____

Day 2 – Focus

The process of discovering our personal identity is one of the most rewarding journeys we will ever take. It's not easy, but when we begin to discover and tap into who we really are, apart from the trappings of our lives, the results will invigorate and empower us.

The process of self-discovery is much like peeling an onion. When we peel an onion we remove one layer at a time until we get to the core, which began as a seed. Like the onion, we all began as a seed, biologically speaking – the seed of life. Our seed carries everything about us, including our unique DNA and our unique identity.

Over time, many layers piled on top of our unique identity, layers of experience, layers of fear, layers of disappointment, and layers of all sorts of things. When we get back to the core of who we are, the seed, we can live life from the healthy place of our true identity. We find out who we truly are and why we are so valuable.

Read Psalm 139:13-16. How does this help us realize our value and worth?

____

____

The issue is that to get there we have to strip away all that we are not. Like peeling an onion, it can be messy and painful. There may be a time we need to step back because our journey of discovery is so intense. Failure to do so will forever bind us to the emptiness of trying to define ourselves according to what we do in life instead of who we are, to what someone did to us or said about us, to circumstances beyond our control, or to what has happened in our past.

Day 3 - Foundation

When we do the work of finding out who we really are, our lives are shaped and shifted in all the best ways. Our identity is not based on what we do, in fact it is totally separate. Our identity comes from God and is revealed in His Word.

Read Isaiah 43:1, 4, and 7. What do you learn about your true identity?

____

____

____

God called us by name, proclaiming we are His. He declares us precious in His sight, honored, loved, and created for His glory. He formed us, made us, we are His. He said it, but many of us are unaware, so we go through life defining ourselves in terms of accomplishments or activities rather than internal realities.

Unfortunately, much of our social system in the United States is built on knowing what people do, not who they are. It happens in our relationships with others as well as our relationship with ourselves. We find it easier to focus on our actions than on our inner beings, so we default to talking about what we do. Who we are and what we do are separate aspects of our lives.

In order to live successful lives, we cannot define ourselves or hope to find our value in what we do – those are all our external qualities. We need to define ourselves and our worth by who we are on the inside. Identity isn't what's readily visible to others, but what God has put deep inside of us, not only our uniqueness as individuals, but also the spiritual realities He has deposited in us as believers.

In order to know who we truly are, we have to perceive the gifts God has given us rightly, so we can draw strength and pursue our destinies based on all He has placed inside of us, not on anything we could gain through human effort.

Read Ephesians 1:3-14. What do we learn about God's gifts to us and our destiny?

____

____

____

____

Our identities are not founded in our circumstances. Our value and self-worth stand firm in our relationship with God. We have to separate who we are from what we do. We must realize who we are is firmly established in our identity in Christ, not in what we do. When we understand, no matter what our circumstances are we can bounce back and do better following a loss or failure. In fact, failure cannot keep us down when we know our true identity. Our "who" in God makes all things possible.

Take a look at your life today. Do you feel important because of what you do or who you are?

____

If you attribute more to your "do" than your "who" you need to determine where you find your identity and make the changes that are needed. When your "who" defines and drives your life, opposition, obstacles, and even unfair treatment are not allowed to become determining factors about who you are.

Day 5 – Journal – Affirmations

As we close our week, journal what you've discovered about how you define your identity.

____

____

____

____

____

Next, write a prayer asking God to help you to peel the onion even further to see your "who" in Him is more important than what you "do" or the circumstances you find yourself in! Ask Him to help you understand your true identity and your value in Him. Close with thanks for all you've learned this week.

____

____

____

____

____

____

Week 42: It's Time to Peel the Onion – Who You Are is Much More Important

Day 1 – Set the Stage

As we continue to peel the onion, we need to realize our identity is not based on what has happened to us. Most of us know the familiar story of King Saul, who was King David's predecessor on the throne of Israel. When God chose David to rule after him, Saul ended up a tormented man who tried on numerous occasions to kill David. One reason David was kind to Saul was because of his friendship with Saul's son, Jonathan.

Years after Saul and Jonathan had died, David remembered his friend and asked, "Is there anyone still left of the house of Saul to whom I can show kindness for Jonathan's sake?" (2 Sam. 9:1). He discovered Jonathan had a son who lived in poverty in Lo-Debar, so he sent for him.

Read 2 Samuel 9:6-8. What did David promise Jonathan's son, Mephibosheth, when they met?

How did Mephibosheth respond?

Clearly, Mephibosheth had an identity problem, believing he lacked value because of what had happened to him and his family. Have you ever felt your value and identity were wrapped tightly in something that had happened to you?

King David offered to completely restore all that his family had lost and treat him as family (moving him to the palace and including him in every meal). Mephibosheth thought so poorly of himself he could not even acknowledge David's grace and favor. All he could focus on was his lowly opinion of himself.

Read 2 Samuel 4:4. Mephibosheth was a prince but what had happened to leave him living in poverty and viewing himself as a "dead dog?"

____

____

Saul's family had been forced to flee, and in their flight from danger, Mephibosheth's nurse tripped and dropped him, and he became crippled. From his story, we can see anyone can lose their sense of identity, even the grandson of a king. The good news is anyone can also regain it.

Regaining our sense of identity means dealing with what happened to us in the past. Bad things happen to people, often tragic and many times outside the victim's control. When bad things happen, we have to choose whether to live with the negative consequences of what others did to us or allowed to happen to us or we can choose to overcome. Many of us can relate. Perhaps something deeply wounded you but it was not your fault, maybe the person who caused the damage didn't intend to hurt you. While you can't change what happened, you can change how it affects you. You have a choice: focus on what happened or focus on who you are. What will you choose?

____

Day 3 – Foundation

Who we are has absolutely nothing to do with what has happened to us. If Mephibosheth had chosen to focus on who he was, he could have experienced restoration much sooner than he did because David had a track record of kindness toward Saul's family. Had he viewed himself as the royalty he was instead of as a "dead dog," his entire life would have been different. What happened to Mephibosheth affected him dramatically, but it did not have to change who he was or how he viewed himself.

If you have struggled with allowing your past to define you, one of the best things you can do is break free from it. You can move beyond the things that have hurt you, handicapped you, or hindered you, and pursue your destiny by remembering these four facts: things happen, freedom comes from forgiveness, "who" you are is much more important than what happened to you, and changing what you can is crucial.

Good things happen to us, so do bad things – it's all part of living. Many times, when circumstances are extremely painful or have caused problems for us, we are tempted to deny them or blame them on other things. The truth is, in most cases, we cannot help what happened to us, we can only decide we will not allow these bad things to define us. We can accept them as part of our life's journey, but refuse to see them as the defining moment of our lives.

Read Ephesians 4:31-32. What are we told to do in regard to those who have hurt us?

____

____

Day 4 – Reflect

No matter who was involved in the tragic or unfortunate things that happened in our past or what their specific roles were, the only way to set ourselves free from them is to forgive them. When we do, freedom, strength, and new perspectives on life will fill our hearts and minds.

Mephibosheth's biggest problem was obsessing about what happened to him instead of embracing who he was and what he could become. He fixed his gaze on what he could not do instead of what he could do.

As we move forward, we have to stay focused on our identity in Christ, not on incidents in our past. In putting past events behind us and forgiving those involved, we can build ourselves up and gain a whole new outlook on life. We have to choose to change what we can change.

In many situations, we give ourselves permission to remain stuck in our pain or disappointment. Even if we can't do what we always wanted to do, we can move forward in life, doing what we can to change our circumstances rather than letting them overcome us. If our past has caused us to believe certain things about our identity that are simply not true, we can have a fresh start with a great life full of good things.

Read Isaiah 43:19. How can God's promise help us have a fresh start?

____

____

All we have to do is realize our "who" is not our "do." Our past is the past; we don't have to take it into our future.

Day 5 – Journal – Affirmations

Let's close this week with a few questions. Be completely honest as you journal your responses.

What are some of the layers you need to peel back in order to reveal your true identity?

____

How would you define your true identity?

____

What is the most valuable discovery you have ever made in finding out who you really are?

____

In your life, what has happened that has become so big it now overshadows who you are? How might you change the way you think about yourself and your true identity in order to put that situation in proper perspective?

____

____

____

In light of today's self-assessment, what areas do you need to ask God to help you? Compose a simple prayer asking for His guidance.

____

____

Week 43: The Best Kept Secret of Sustained Success – Success Can Be Fleeting

Day 1 – Set the Stage

Irving Berlin, the famous American composer and songwriter said, "The toughest thing about success is that you've got to keep on being a success." He was right! Some people seem to know exactly what to do to reach the pinnacle of success, but they know little about how to stay there once they do. Sometimes others may be responsible for their downfall, but most of the time they can only blame themselves. Some people fail to succeed; others succeed only to become very successful at failure.

The internal dynamics needed to reach a point of success are different from those required to stay successful. Reaching a goal often takes one set of skills and personal resources, while living with success after achieving goals requires an entirely different set of skills and resources.

Read Proverbs 22:2. What can we surmise about success from this verse?

____

____

____

____

All success comes from God. When we know who we truly are in Him and truly understand all gifts come from Him – including success – we can achieve and sustain true success even though here on earth it seems success can be fleeting.

Day 2 – Focus

We know success isn't necessarily permanent. From Xerxes I of Persia to Jimmy Swaggart, from Lance Armstrong to Leona Helmsley, we have seen seemingly successful people suffer because personal weakness took them from the pinnacle of success to total disgrace.

These individuals reached great heights of success and then fell, but the same dynamics that toppled them are the basic reasons why other, less well-known people have the potential to succeed, yet never do. Among us there may be those who yearn for success and significance, only to sabotage themselves time and time again. Maybe it's happening to one or more of us, though there seems to be no reason we can't live the life we long for, but every time we pursue our purpose, we get derailed. It may even happen repeatedly. Be encouraged – we can identify, understand, and solve the problem, breaking through the barriers which have blocked us from the greatness we were born to enjoy.

Read John 3:27. What does John the Baptist mean here?

____

____

____

____

Essentially, John says it is not possible for a person to succeed without heaven's help. Everything, every ability, every position is God's gift. If we are to be defined as successful it is because God has granted us the ability to be successful.

People have tumbled from positions of prominence to the depths of obscurity for centuries. Influential voices have been silenced because they got caught up in corruption; people of certain socioeconomic status have lost their wealth; a haughty socialite or an arrogant leader has been humbled. It happened to the first king of the nation of Israel, a thirty-year-old man named Saul. Known early on as tall and handsome and later regarded as a shrewd and victorious military leader, Saul preceded David as king, and like David, King Saul experienced remarkable success but only to a point. Samuel, the priest and prophet, anointed Saul as king, giving Saul a series of instructions about what he needed to do as the nation's new leader.

Read 1 Samuel 10:8. What was one of Samuel's instructions to Saul?

____

____

Read 1 Samuel 13:8-14. Did Saul obey Samuel's instruction?

____

____

What was the result?

____

____

Saul went to Gilgal, but when Samuel did not arrive seven days later, Saul acted foolishly and offered a sacrifice. As quickly as Saul gained God's favor, he lost it, forfeiting everything God had for him.

Yesterday we watched Saul lose his destiny, failing to maintain his position of success. What flaws did you see which caused him to lose his success?

____

____

____

____

He had a bad habit of making excuses (he didn't take responsibility for his actions). He was impatient (because of his perspective). He was disobedient (but God was gracious to Saul – as He nearly always is – allowing us to try again because He wants us to succeed). He compared himself to another (David) and allowed himself to become jealous. He was fearful (Saul knew the presence of the Lord had left him and he could tell God's presence and favor were upon David). He was proud (too proud to acknowledge David's victories or to honor David for them). One of the saddest aspects of Saul's story is that he could have succeeded.

Saul lived centuries ago, but we can see these same weaknesses causing people today to struggle. Which, if any, of these flaws can you identify in your own life and in your quest for success?

____

____

____

____

Day 5 – Journal – Affirmations

As we close this week, let's give Saul credit where credit is due. He was one of the greatest figures of human history. He was tall, good-looking, and well-liked, baptized into the Spirit of God. His lineage was filled with great historical figures like Abraham, Israel, and Moses. Saul united a people, founded a kingdom, and created an army, something few men have ever done. He won battles in the power of God. He was a prophet - the Spirit came on him in power. He was everything people today are seeking - empowered with the Holy Spirit and able to do the impossible for God. In light of these truths what do you need to talk to God about? Write your prayer here.

Week 44: The Best Kept Secret of Sustained Success – The Keys to Sustain Success

Day 1 – Set the Stage

Last week, we learned about Saul, his greatness, his weaknesses, and his downfall. This week, let's learn how not to be like Saul as we seek the keys to sustained success. So many of us struggle with the same issues which caused Saul to lose his position and his destiny. If we are honest, we can remember times in which we have been irresponsible, impatient, or disobedient. We can also think of situations in which we have been afraid, compared ourselves with others and become jealous of them, and walked in pride instead of humility.

Some of us manage these behaviors better than others. Some manage most of them well, but we still find ourselves in a seemingly constant battle. For example, some of us are not impatient, but are irresponsible. Others are not easily jealous, but battle fear in every situation.

The key to sustained success is to resolve our issues (weaknesses) as quickly as we can as soon as we recognize them. Otherwise, like Saul, we will be people of tremendous potential and promise, but lose everything. Thankfully, our stories can be accounts of increasing strength and victory, not continual weakness and defeat.

Read Ephesians 6:10. What are we, as believers, commanded to do?

____

____

____

Day 2 – Focus

Being irresponsible is easy. Taking responsibility is more difficult, but it is vital to long-term success. If you struggle with irresponsibility, look for areas in which you can start small and improve.

For example, we can all take responsibility for managing our time. We don't have to rely on someone else to wake us but can set our own alarm. We can also take responsibility for our health by making healthy food choices, disciplining ourselves to exercise, and keeping doctor's appointments as recommended. Each of these are simple ways we can grow in our capacity to be responsible. Learning to take responsibility is a stepping-stone to success.

Read James 1:22. How does this verse relate to taking responsibility?

____

We are instructed to do what the Word says – there is no greater responsibility.

Being patient is another key to sustaining success. So many of us sabotage our own success because we are not willing to wait. When we are moving toward new levels of greatness, we may get ahead of ourselves, but often, success is a matter of timing – just because it doesn't happen when we want it to doesn't mean it will never happen. We need to discipline ourselves to be patient as we strive for success.

Read Psalm 37:7. What promise is implied if we follow the instructions?

____

____

Day 3 – Foundation

We need to be obedient. We saw Saul's disobedience was his biggest mistake.

Read Luke 5:4-7. What happens when the disciples obeyed Jesus?

____

____

____

This is just one example of the principle "obedience leads to blessing" which we see repeated throughout Scripture. As long as Saul obeyed God, he enjoyed God's blessing. When he stopped, it all fell apart. That same pattern is still in effect today and applies directly to us. God will always lead us in the best possible way to the best possible results, even if we don't like or understand the process. Anytime He asks for our obedience, we can be certain it is for our good.

We also need to resist fear. The older Saul got, the more fearful he became. His fears sucked the greatness out of him.

Read Isaiah 41:10. What is commanded? What does God promise?

____

____

____

Feeling afraid is a normal part of life, but allowing fear to control us, to override our sensibilities, to keep us from doing what we know we should do, or to cause us to hold back when we need to move forward is a big problem. Few emotions will block success and shut down a journey to greatness like fear!

Day 4 – Reflect

Take responsibility. Be patient. Be obedient. Do not fear. Resist comparison and jealousy. Too often, we look to see how what we are doing stacks up to what others are doing. Jealousy and comparison have their roots in selfishness and pride, and there is no end to what a jealous person will find to envy about others.

Read 1 Corinthians 3:3. What is the warning?

____

____

____

Mature believers are secure in who they are and are able to honor and enjoy the successes of others, without a twinge of jealousy, encouraging them to go after their dreams and fulfill their potential. They know who they are, their identities are established, and they have conquered selfishness and pride.

Charles Spurgeon said to be humble, is "to make a right estimate of oneself." Many of us have been taught humility means not standing up for ourselves, choosing weakness over strength, or becoming a doormat - none of which is true. Genuine humility requires an accurate assessment of ourselves, an honest evaluation of both our strengths and weaknesses. It requires a respectful expression of who we really are—not a suppression of our true selves in an effort to please or defer to someone else for the sake of keeping peace. To practice humility is not to refuse to act or to keep your mouth shut, but to act and speak wisely, respectfully, and truthfully whenever a situation calls for it.

Day 5 – Journal – Affirmations

When we achieve a level of success, it is not guaranteed to last. It can only be sustained if we are willing to work at it. While there are certain external duties that must be fulfilled in order to stay successful, the most important obligations are internal and include taking the responsibilities our roles require; managing negative emotions like impatience, fear, and jealousy; being humble before God; and living a lifestyle of obedience to Him. God has tremendous success in store for us—more than we could ever ask for or imagine (Eph. 3:20).

As we close our week, let's journal our affirmations, concerns, and prayers, based on what we learned.

Week 45: Success is an Inside Job – The Identity/Courage Connection

Day 1 – Set the Stage

Courage is a powerful word, isn't it? It's powerful not only because it evokes images of bravery and boldness, but also because it's something we all wish we had in abundance! Deep inside, we long to be more courageous than we are. We know courage could be the key to living our dreams but the real reason we don't go after our dreams with the passion we'd like is because we are afraid we might fail. We come up with all kinds of reasons to talk ourselves out of pursuing our dreams, but at the end of the day these "reasons" are nothing more than fears - fear of failure, fear of inadequacy, fear of what other people will think about us, fear of lack, fear that the future will not be what we had hoped, or fear of countless other things.

Read 2 Timothy 1:7. What do you learn about fear?

____

____

____

We want to be strong, both in the way we present ourselves to other people and the way we think about ourselves. Society tells us admitting our fears is not strong so we suppress them, talk around them, and put other labels on them. We avoid at all costs saying, "I'm afraid . . ." But the truth is, as difficult as it is to admit, the reason many of us live only wishing we could do certain things instead of doing them is we lack courage. From 2 Timothy 1:7, we know our timidity is not from God, so what should we do?

It is clear we do not know what to do with the fears and doubts that arise when we think about pursuing our dreams. The difference between those who only wish for greatness and those who go on to achieve success and sustain it is those who reach it are able to manage the fear-based internal issues they face along the way. Courage is non-negotiable for anyone who wants to follow a dream or achieve success.

Courage is an ancient word with roots in French and Latin words which mean "heart." A modern definition of the word is, "mental or moral strength to venture, persevere, and withstand danger, fear, or difficulty." An older, fuller definition from the 1913 edition of Webster's dictionary describes courage as "that quality of mind which enables one to encounter dangers and difficulty with firmness, or without fear, or fainting of heart; valor, boldness, resolution." We can see from these definitions that courage is an intensely internal personal quality.

People can certainly encourage us, but they can't force us to be courageous. We have to find courage within ourselves, and the sooner we do, the sooner we will find ourselves living the lives we have only imagined.

Read Luke 12:32. Jesus says, "Do not be afraid, little flock..." Why? How can this encourage you to be more courageous in the pursuit of your dreams?

____

____

____

____

Day 3 – Foundation

What then is the connection between identity and courage? Do you see it yet? Courage comes from within us and can't be faked. Sometimes we say, "I have to put my game face on," meaning we want to appear focused, determined, and poised for victory in some sort of competition or business dealing. While our game face may fool or intimidate an opponent, it is only skin deep. The difference between those who only wish for greatness and those who go on to achieve and sustain greatness is those who reach it are able to manage well the internal issues they face along the way.

Those who have true courage rooted deep in who they are don't need a game face – they live with confidence and boldness every day, in every situation because it's part of who they are. The only way to be truly courageous is to live your life based on your true identity.

Read Mark 6:50. Why could the disciples be courageous? Why can we be courageous?

____

____

____

They were terrified, but Jesus encouraged them to be courageous because He was with them. The same is true for us! Trying to drum up courage any other way simply will not work. Courage is the opposite of fear and it is what we need to deal with our fears. Fear is the fruit of misplaced identity. Because our identity is in Christ we can be courageous and strong as we go after our true destiny.

Day 4 – Reflect

When we become established in our identities, fear will flee and courage will come. We need to know who we are and have a solid understanding that we have value and potential apart from our environment and the people from our past, only then can we move forward and reach our goals.

Read Numbers 13:17-33. Moses had just led the Israelites out of slavery in Egypt. Here, he sends spies to check out the land God had promised them – a rich land flowing with milk and honey. What was the majority report?

____

____

After a 40 day expedition, the men acknowledged the milk and honey, but they had more to say about the enemies who inhabited the land than about anything else. Caleb, one of the spies, spoke up saying, "We should go up and take possession of the land, for we can certainly do it." Why was his report so different from the others?

____

____

They doubted God and were instantly afraid, not wanting to take the land God had given them. Caleb, on the other hand, trusted the Lord wholeheartedly and took Him at His Word, and Joshua agreed with Him.

Where are you standing in your journey to your promised land?

____

____

Day 5 – Journal – Affirmations

As we close this week, journal your fears, then ask God to give you the courage you need to overcome them and make the identity/courage connection as you pursue your dreams.

____

____

____

____

____

____

____

____

____

____

____

____

Week 46: Success is an Inside Job – You Can Live Your Dream
Day 1 – Set the Stage

We can live our dream whether it is an experience we hope to have or something we want to become! We all have a dream in our hearts - the thought of which makes us feel awesome. Our dreams are often huge and we have to work toward them as we hear the whisper within, "You were made for this!" We may view our dreams as our destiny, our purpose for living, or even as a promise from God. However we frame it, we need to go for it. What is the life you've imagined for yourself? When you really think about what you want out of life, what do you see?

____

____

____

____

Some of us can answer quickly and definitively, others need time to ponder the answers.

Read Proverbs 16:9. How does this verse encourage you to pursue your dreams?

____

____

Once our dream is established in our hearts, we need to move toward it with confidence as we allow the Lord to establish our steps in other words, we need to dream the dreams we want to live, and allow God to make us able to live them.

Day 2 – Focus

Some of us have let disappointments and delays cause us to doubt our dreams. There's no shame or condemnation in it at all – it happens to the best of dreamers. We all encounter naysayers and discouragers. Sometimes they are the people we are closest to and would least expect, and it is painful. It takes courage to stand up to them.

Whether you are just now beginning to think about your dream or whether you need to commit afresh to your pursuit of it, it's time to move forward toward your dream. Your promise or dream is worth pursuing. Someone once said, "No dreamer is ever too small; no dream is ever too big." Your dream can never be too big, especially when it's a dream God has placed in your heart.

Read Romans 8:31-32. How does God's Word encourage you in your dream?

____

____

____

____

Last week, we learned how Joshua and Caleb were able to adopt God's big dream for Israel as their own. There is something we need to understand as we go after our big dreams – they won't come easily and challenges are to be expected. Knowing these truths ahead of time can help us be prepared for the challenges and ready to overcome them with God's help. As God's Word promises, "If God is for us, who can be against us?"

Day 3 – Foundation

The fulfillment of our dreams one day will be incredible. We need to be willing to work toward our dreams, be innovative in their pursuit, and be patient as those dreams come to pass. Difficulties don't invalidate our dreams. Remember whatever you move toward, moves toward you.

So, this time next year, or ten years from now, who do you want to be and what do you want to be doing with your life? (You won't become your job, your house, your car, or any of your possessions, but you will become your dream.) As you consider this question, don't make excuses about why your dream can't happen or complain about the obstacles in your way. Rather, think about the ways you can make your dreams happen because of all the potential inside you!

____

____

____

Read Philippians 4:13. How does this verse encourage your dream?

____

____

Read it again in the Amplified Bible, "I can do all things [which He has called me to do] through Him who strengthens and empowers me [to fulfill His purpose—I am self-sufficient in Christ's sufficiency; I am ready for anything and equal to anything through Him who infuses me with inner strength and confident peace.]" Do you need to change your answer?

Day 4 – Reflect

Our dreams are worth protecting from being forgotten and never coming true. A dream can be fragile, and one way to protect it is to keep it in the forefront of our mind every day. Whether it means putting a photo to represent the dream on our screensaver or a note on our mirror, we have to make sure we remain mentally aware of it – taking steps toward it regularly. The steps don't have to be big or dramatic; but they do need to be intentional. We have to take deliberate steps to remind us of our dream and move us in the right direction. What is one step you can take this week to keep your dream alive?

Another way we must protect our dream is by sharing it wisely. The temptation is to tell everyone about our dream and expect them to be as excited as we are. Sadly, some people simply are not mature enough to support other people's dreams and aspirations because of their own insecurities. They may even be jealous and critical. When we have a dream, we should share it only with people who have proven themselves to be on our side, people who will encourage us, affirm us, and help our dream come true. Who can you trust with your dream?

Finally, we need to have the discipline to fight for our dreams. As we go after our dreams, we will face obstacles, but we can't let them discourage us and make us give up. Instead we need to use our time, energy, and finances wisely because making our dream a priority will likely require sacrifice. What will you do this week with your time, energy, or finances to make your dream a reality?

Day 5 – Journal – Affirmations

As we close our week, answer this question, "Where do you need God's help in living your dream?" Write a short prayer asking for His help and guidance to help you attain your God-given dreams.

____

____

____

____

____

Read the following verses and write a personal affirmation from each one based on God's Word to us.

Psalm 18:30-33

____

____

____

Jeremiah 29:11-13

____

____

____

Week 47: The Journey to Significance – Attention Seeking Versus True Significance

Day 1 – Set the Stage

When we are unsure of our identity, we tend to crave attention and not always the good kind. Sometimes our attempts to get attention are annoying, other times foolish, and sometimes even dangerous. The truth is most attention seeking is really an attempt at fulfilling our need for significance.

Read Genesis 29. What do you learn about Leah?

____

____

____

____

Like each of us, Leah wanted to be noticed and loved, she craved the genuine, God-given need for significance. It isn't a problem unless we try to meet that need in unhealthy or destructive ways. When our identity is in question, we seek attention. When we are aware of our identity in Christ, we seek the significance only God can give.

Leah must have felt rejected, married off to Jacob through trickery because her father feared no one would choose her. Jacob felt no love for her, only her sister, Rachel. Imagine the pain she felt because she was in love with Jacob. God wants to communicate His truths to each of us who are searching for real significance through the story of Leah. This week we will discover what God has for us as we study the life of Leah.

Read Genesis 29:17. How is Leah described?

____

____

Described as weak-eyed and dull, Leah was well aware Jacob did not want her. God's Word doesn't tell us why she didn't speak up in the bedchamber on her wedding night, but it is possible that deep down she wanted to know what it felt like to be significant and loved. It seems she took her one chance at feeling loved.

Read Genesis 29:31. What did the Lord see? What did He do on her behalf?

____

____

____

We can conclude Leah lived as one who felt profoundly rejected and unloved. Even so, she fell in love with Jacob, but he never fell in love with her. Compared to the love he showered on her sister Rachel, she likely felt hated due to the complete lack of love and affection. Leah was on what seemed a futile search for significance which lasted for years. Have you ever felt that way?

____

Interestingly, God opened her womb and she began to bear children. Her search for significance is evident in the names she chose for them beginning with her firstborn, Reuben, whose name means "see a son." When pronounced in Hebrew Rueben even sounds like "He has seen me."

Day 3 – Foundation

Feeling invisible is painful for anyone. When we hope someone will notice us and they don't, we can understand how Leah felt. In some cases, we may be oversensitive and feel rejected when we are not being rejected at all, but in Leah's situation, Jacob truly overlooked and ignored her most of the time. It hurt Leah centuries ago and it hurts everyone who feels that way today.

In her search for significance, Leah wanted to be seen. The same is true for anyone who is searching for significance. Read the following verses and note the names of her children and their meaning in relation to her search for significance.

Genesis 29:33 ____

Genesis 29:34 ____

Genesis 29:35 ____

Simeon means "to hear." Leah desperately wanted to be heard. She named her third son, Levi, which means "joined" or "connected." In addition to wanting to be seen and heard, Leah also wanted to be connected. She wanted to feel that she was not alone. She hadn't been successful, but now she hoped the connection she longed for would finally fall into place. We can all relate, there are times the connection we long for isn't happening and we seek attention, trying to work harder, doing the right things, and changing ourselves to be significant to those who aren't even paying attention!

The good news is from a spiritual perspective, our connection with God is established and we are significant to Him.

Day 4 – Reflect

Let's read the following verses and note what we learn about our significance to God and in His Kingdom.

Matthew 10:29-31

Each of us is significant in God's eyes. Here we see our significance demonstrated in the fact that the details of our lives are not only known to God but valuable.

Ephesians 2:10

Not only are we significant to God but so are our gifts and abilities. We are created with both purpose and intention to do the work God has prepared for us to do.

Isaiah 43:7

God created each of us uniquely for a specific purpose, bringing glory to Him. We are created with intention and significance. We can have confidence in our significance and the impact we can have for God – we don't need to seek attention. In fact, from a human perspective, the divine connections God has for us don't require the effort we put in when we continually seek attention. Whenever God wants us to join our life with someone else's there is grace, ease, and peace. God makes it happen for us with real significance and without the need for attention seeking.

As we close our week, take a few minutes to journal any affirmations, thoughts, or prayers, based on what we have learned this week regarding your significance and what God wants you to do with your new found wisdom.

Week 48: The Journey to Significance – The Significance Only God Can Give

Day 1 – Set the Stage

Last week, we met Leah who was on her own journey to significance. Her name comes from the Hebrew word meaning "weary" – a fact that is both interesting and sad. We know Leah grew weary wanting to be seen, heard, and connected in an intimate relationship. She worked for years to no avail. No matter how hard she tried, every effort left her alone, ignored, disregarded, and devalued. Exerting that kind of emotional and relational energy is more draining than any physical effort.

The kind of efforts Leah made – and so many of us make today – leave our soul depleted. Physical rest cannot solve the problem of an empty, barren soul; it takes a supernatural healing touch. How many times have you struggled to be seen or heard, or to connect with people in a meaningful way and wound up weary?

____

____

The search for significance can be exhausting, but it doesn't have to be. When we look for value in the wrong places, we end up weary like Leah. Yet, when our search takes us in the right direction, we find ourselves rested, restored, and renewed. If you have worn yourself out trying to feel significant, you do not have to stay tired and frustrated.

Read Acts 3:19. From what/whom do times of refreshing come?

____

____

Day 2 – Focus

We learned in Acts 3:19 yesterday that the key to the most meaningful rest we will ever know comes from the presence of the Lord when we repent of our sins. The word repent means "to change one's mind" and it applies especially "to acceptance of the will of God." God's will for us as His sons and daughters is to find our significance in Him alone and to allow Him to create in us a strong sense of identity.

Read 2 Corinthians 5:21. What do you think this verse says about our significance?

____

____

____

____

Here, Paul proclaims Christ took on our sin so we could become the righteousness of God, in other words, so we would be made acceptable and put in a right relationship with Him. We need to build on our identity in Christ a greater awareness of our intrinsic value and worth, not based on anything we can do for ourselves, but on what His Son has already done for us.

He has saved us, redeemed us, healed us, set us free, and made us more than conquerors. He has incredible plans for us that will lead us to the significance we long for! There's a big difference between seeking attention and searching for significance. All we have to do is stop looking for value in what or who is around us and realize our search ends in His great love.

Day 3 - Foundation

By now, we can all clearly see the difference between fame/attention and success/significance. For those who seek true significance in life, attention alone is never enough.

Compare the lives of any of today's celebrities with Helen Keller. She lived a successful life and her success was inseparable from her significance though she was never famous in the sense of a modern celebrity. The paparazzi never ran after her the way they chase countless celebrities today. Her everyday life did not capture people's attention; her contributions to humanity did. People were curious about her ability to lead a meaningful, productive life despite her obstacles.

The right kind of attention from the right people goes a long way toward helping us feel significant and understand our value, but it can't completely fill a significance gap in our hearts - only God can!

Read Genesis 29:35. What seemed to have changed for Leah?

____

____

She named her fourth son Judah which means "praise." It seems Leah had finally learned the Lord was the only one who could make her truly significant. She looked to God and worshipped Him, finally understanding what she had missed all along. God had been paying attention to her all along and He loved her as He always had. She was seen, heard, and connected by God and praised Him for it! Are you there yet?

____

Day 4 – Reflect

Leah represents those of us who feel we must earn our right standing before God by performing well enough.

Read Ephesians 2:8-9. Is it possible to earn our right standing before God? Why or why not?

Not a single one of us can do anything to earn God's love. It's a gift. We can't work for it; we simply receive it—and then we praise the Lord out of grateful hearts that finally know the truth.

Did you ever think that perhaps the best thing God has done in your life is to close certain doors of opportunity, to keep you away from certain relationships, or to say "no" or "not yet" to dreams you were bursting in anticipation to see come true?

It's likely the greatest thing God has done for you is to isolate you for a season. Why? Only when we reach a point of disappointment and can we say, "God, I realize You are my only hope. This time, I will praise the Lord. I am significant to You." Have you reached the point where you understand if all you ever have in life is Jesus, He is enough? This is the place where you live for God and God alone.

Day 5 - Journal - Affirmations

God knows most of us have spent a great deal of time looking for acknowledgment, acceptance, and approval from other people who have never given us a chance. As we close this week - let this be our affirmation:

Everything they failed to do for us — God will do.

Every time they turned their heads away from us — God turned His head in our direction.

When other people don't see us — God does.

He is the One who will do for us much more than they ever will.

He is able to do immeasurably more than all we ask or imagine, according to his power that is at work within us...(Ephesians 3:30-21).

God's eye is on us, and not only can He meet our deepest needs and desires, He can do even more than we can imagine.

Feel free to add more based on what God has spoken to your hearts this week.

Love

Week 49: I Love You This Much – The Greatest Demonstration of Love

Day 1 – Set the Stage

Søren Kierkegaard, Danish theologian, poet, philosopher, and author sought happiness with God. He pursued his relationship with God with such intensity his writing always centered around the warm and personal love of God. He urged his audience to let go of their empty religious practices to instead pursue a real, authentic, and tender relationship with a living, loving God.

In 1847, Kierkegaard wrote *Works of Love* in which he declared, "Deep within every man there lies the dread of being alone in the world, forgotten by God, overlooked among the household of millions upon millions."

He believed the answer to aloneness was love because love binds us to God and each other and saves us from isolation.

Read 1 John 4:15-19. What do you learn about God's great love for us?

____

____

____

____

When we love God because He first loved us, then our lives will manifest this incredible love and this kind of love will be eternal.

Kierkegaard's intense and lasting love affair with God reflected the kind of relationship God had with Noah, Abraham, Moses, and David. Each believed in God, obeyed God, and loved God. None of them were perfect human beings, but each was passionate about his relationship with God.

The people of Israel were not always as faithful, falling into a repetitive cycle of love given (by God), love rejected (by the people), and, finally, love accepted (through a covenant relationship).

Read Deuteronomy 9:1-24 and Deuteronomy 32:1-43 for two of the many examples of this. Do you see the pattern?

Not only is this cycle of love on display between God and Israel throughout the Old Testament but also in troubled relationships all around us, all the time. One person offers another person love, but the other person doesn't reciprocate with love and the relationship falls apart. Sometimes, the one who rejected the initial gesture has a change of heart and tries to revive the relationship, offering love to try to resurrect the other's feelings. Sometimes love is fully accepted, and the relationship grows into something beautiful and healthy. Other times it turns into an unhealthy cycle of love offered and rejected on both sides, over and over, repeatedly hurting both parties.

Through these cycles with Israel, God maintained His love. He cared for His people, always desiring a close and affectionate relationship with them even when their hearts grew cold and their love for Him all but died out.

Day 3 – Foundation

During these cycles, God kept on loving His people and, finally, after many, many cycles of love given-rejected-accepted, God sent to His people the ultimate display of His love and affection—His Son, Jesus Christ. Jesus' arrival on earth and what He accomplished here is the greatest demonstration of love the world has ever seen.

Jesus was and is the tangible expression of God's overwhelming, staggering, and outright crazy love for us. With Jesus everything changed, including the covenants. With Jesus there was a new covenant, a different kind of covenant.

Read Hebrews 7:18-22. What kind of covenant was ushered in by Jesus?

____

With the arrival of Jesus came the better covenant, a grant covenant relationship with God, where He does all the work, but also the death and resurrection of Jesus is the greatest example of God's love the world has ever seen.

Read Matthew 1:1. When did the new era begin?

____

____

It begins in Matthew, the first book of the New Testament. It is easy to detect the specific connection between Jesus and the new covenant, and the covenants of Abraham and David. Jesus the Messiah was the son of Abraham and the son of David. In other words, Jesus was the living fulfillment of the promises made to Abraham and David.

Day 4 – Reflect

When Jesus appeared on the scene, the people of Israel were still bound and living under the multitude of old, stifling laws and rules of the Mosaic covenant. The relationship with God must have felt like a whole lot of work, with their failure to keep the laws inevitable. No human being alive could keep every single detailed law in the Old Testament Scriptures.

Not only were the laws difficult to learn and to keep, but the religious leaders were constantly creating new rules, and new subsets of rules, for the people to obey. God's chosen people were relating to God in terms of obedience to an impossible-to-keep set of laws. Their failure was guaranteed.

It can be the same today when churches or other religious organizations create sets of rules, and subsets of rules, for people to follow. Those who grow up in those kinds of restrictive religious systems sometimes picture God as an old cranky man in the sky making up rules and punishing people who don't follow the rules – after all it is the only picture of God to which they are exposed. They're relating and responding to an old system. It's defunct.

Read Hebrews 8:7-13. How does God describe the new covenant?

____

____

____

There's a game changer on the scene, and His name is Jesus. When you try to live by the law, it never works.

Day 5 – Journal – Affirmations

As we close this week, write a short prayer thanking God for the greatest demonstration of love – Jesus Christ.

Week 50: I Love You This Much – The New Covenant

Day 1 – Set the Stage

In Hebrews 8:10, God proclaims the new covenant, "I will put my laws in their minds and write them on their hearts. I will be their God, and they will be my people." With the new covenant centered around Jesus, we work from God's love, not for it. The new covenant is based on God's love, a powerful, passionate love that is unchanging, unending, and unconditional. The moment any person, religious leader, or system begins to put restrictions on God's love, he or she is heading down an incorrect and obsolete path, because there's a new path created by the life and work of Jesus.

There is great power in how the genealogy of Jesus traces back to David and Abraham. Jesus is the fulfillment of the promise made to Abraham and David – which is part of the reason we have a grant-covenant relationship with God. The program changed with the arrival of Jesus – the old ways of thinking about God and the law would never be the same. Jesus' death on the cross and His resurrection removed the penalty and punishment of never being able to live up to the law.

Read Jeremiah 31:31-33. How does the new covenant differ from the old one?

____

____

When we're no longer living under the burden and conviction of the law, we can move on from the Mosaic covenant (the old covenant), and live and move and breathe in the new-covenant promise of a firsthand, personal relationship with God through Jesus Christ.

Day 2 – Focus

In the new covenant we're back to a grant relationship with God, where He does the work, forging a relationship with us because He loves us and wants our love. The new covenant under Jesus Christ is a whole new kind of law—the law of love - and it is a face-to-face, intimate, soul-deep relationship.

Read John 1:14. We identified the Word earlier in our study. Who is the Word and what did He do?

Jesus, the Word, put on a human body with all its flaws and came down to live with His people in close community. What a contrast it was from God appearing in a cloud or fire or staying up on a mountain and handing down laws on stone tablets.

Jesus' life changed the game once and for all as He lived and worked and socialized with His people. He loved His friends, old and new, and responded with the love of the Father to everyone He met, rich or poor, slave or free, sinner or outcast. Jesus was God on display, living out the love of His father for all the world to see. Not everyone saw Him and accepted His love, but some did.

Likewise, today not everyone sees Him and accepts His love either, but some do.

Day 3 – Foundation

Søren Kierkegaard never gave up on his relationship with God. Through his study and his writing he came to a strong and abiding understanding of God's love and forgiveness. One of his most famous quotes says, "God turns sinners into saints."

Kierkegaard knew well the cycle of love and rejection and in the end, God's love gave him hope where he once had none. "Never cease loving a person, and never give up hope," he wrote, "love that has grown cold can kindle."

Jesus is the ultimate demonstration of "never cease loving." He was and is the love of God given to us, and the love of God on display.

Read John 3:16-17. What do these verses mean to you?

____

____

____

God's love is for the entire world, and He gave His only Son for that world—the same world which rejected Him. God never stops loving us and never gives up hope that we will return His love. His love never grows cold. His love is always there, warm and waiting for an opportunity to rekindle the passion and restore the relationship. Though we forget Him or push Him away, He is still lovestruck by us. He always will be.

Read Romans 5:8. How does God manifest His great love for us?

____

____

We are desired by God.

Day 4 – Reflect

If you've ever been rejected in a love relationship, how did you cope? Did you turn your love toward someone, or something, else?

____

____

Have you ever been in a cycle of love with God? Have you ever turned away from His love? What brought you back?

____

____

When you think about Jesus and His death and resurrection, do you see a picture of love in it?

____

____

Think about your relationship with God in the past. In your heart, mind, and spirit, did you operate more from rules and laws, or love?

____

____

What Jesus accomplished on earth is the greatest demonstration of love ever seen. Because of the life, death, and resurrection of Jesus, we return to a grant-covenant relationship with God where He does all the work and we don't have to relate to Him through a set of rules. With Jesus, we relate to God through a relationship.

Day 5 – Journal – Affirmations

The new covenant centered around Jesus, which means we work from God's love; we don't work for it. Jesus fulfilled the promises God made to Abraham and David in the ancient but beautiful grant covenants. The new covenant under Jesus is based on a new kind of law—the law of love.

As we close our week, journal your affirmations regarding the greatest demonstration of love, your thoughts on the new covenant, and your prayers thanking God for the law of love.

Week 51: More Than Enough – Hunger for Love, Yearning for Fulfillment

Day 1 – Set the Stage

Mother Teresa famously stated, "The hunger for love is much more difficult to remove than the hunger for bread." Do you remember the last time you were truly hungry? Describe it.

____

____

Your stomach was empty. Your innards were growling. It's always an uncomfortable feeling. When you're hungry or thirsty, it's hard to think about anything except finding the food to fill your stomach or water to quench your thirst. Both hunger and thirst are powerful driving forces, and the hungrier or thirstier you get, the stronger the compulsion to eat or drink something, anything, grows to make it stop.

People around the world fight with similar obsessions, seeking fulfillment through alcohol, drugs, shopping, gambling, or pornography. Even coffee can be a common addiction. The pursuit of wealth and worldly success is another appetite that is hard to tame. Often people spend much of their lives going after things instead of going after God. When they get to the end of their lives, they realize everything without Him is really nothing. The food pantry is bare, the fancy paper coffee cup is empty, but the desire for more is still there.

People living during the time of Jesus had all the common cravings we have. Just like us, they could never get enough to really be happy.

Day 2 – Focus

Since He was fully God and fully human, Jesus felt cravings too. He understood extreme hunger and thirst. One day He showed up at a well in the region of Samaria, both hungry and thirsty.

Read John 4:4-25. Write a brief summary of what happened?

____

____

____

____

____

It was the noon hour, and Jesus sat at the well, tired and waiting, as a woman arrived to draw water. "Would you give me a drink of water?" He asked politely.

The Samaritan woman, taken aback, asked, "How come you, a Jew, are asking me, a Samaritan woman, for a drink?"

In those days Jewish people wouldn't be caught dead talking to Samaritan people. Two thousand years ago, people also struggled with biases and prejudices. Racism and judgmentalism were alive and well. Ten kinds of prejudice have been identified including racial, sexual, chronological, geographical, educational, financial, physical, denominational, ministerial, and doctrinal. These prejudices are bad, but what is even worse is they all have oozed their way into the church. Racism is currently one of the most difficult and painful challenges we face.

Day 3 – Foundation

There is no prejudice in Christ. The Jesus many of us think we know is a Jesus of our own making. We have constructed an image of Him from various experiences, failures, and victories. The problem is the Jesus we have constructed is different from the Jesus who really existed. We'll never penetrate the world with the good news until the good news first penetrates our hearts and minds.

Regardless of what the Jews thought of the Samaritans, Jesus brought a message of grace and went after the woman at the well like the Good Shepherd goes after the lost sheep. Not only did Jesus go after her, but He also went ahead of her, because He got to the well before she did. He was waiting for her to get there, and He couldn't wait to talk to her. Not only was it unusual for a Jewish person to be talking to a Samaritan, but talking to a woman in public was also frowned upon.

Read Galatians 3:28-29. Jesus continually demonstrated this principle – what does it say?

____

____

Jesus did what He always did – rising above the stereotypes and demonstrating all are one in Him. He answered the woman offering a hint of His identity, and a significant but mysterious promise. "If you knew the generosity of God and who I am, you would be asking me for a drink, and I would give you fresh, living water." What did He mean?

____

Day 4 – Reflect

Yesterday we read Jesus words to the Samaritan woman, "If you knew the generosity of God and who I am, you would be asking me for a drink, and I would give you fresh, living water."

She was intrigued, "Sir, you don't even have a bucket to draw with, and this well is deep. So how are you going to get this 'living water'? Are you a better man than our ancestor Jacob, who dug this well and drank from it, he and his sons and livestock, and passed it down to us?"

Jesus didn't hesitate but rather explained something incredible. The living water is an unconditional gift, one that didn't need to be earned.

Reread John 4:13-15. What did they discuss? Did she want what Jesus offered?

____

____

____

____

She believed Jesus and wanted the living water He offered, knowing it would change her life. As their conversation continued, her past came to light - five husbands and currently living with a man to whom she was not married – and Jesus called her out on it. Yet even then, Jesus continued the discussion with her. There was no condemnation from Him as He responded to her hunger for the truth. The thirsty woman daring to approach Jesus is a picture of many of us, yearning for fulfillment. She'd been looking for fulfillment everywhere, except from the one true, living God.

Day 5 - Journal - Affirmations

As we close this week, take a look at your life - are you pursuing happiness and fulfillment from activities, people, and material goods that can never satisfy or are you seeking fulfillment from the one perfect source - Jesus Christ?

____

____

____

As you journal this week, write what God has taught you and what He wants you to do in light of His teaching.

____

____

____

____

____

____

____

____

____

Week 52: More Than Enough – Victory in Jesus

Day 1 – Set the Stage

Many of us have struggled with finding fulfillment, contentment, and peace. It is a common problem today as people seek fame and fortune believing it brings happiness, satisfaction, and significance.

In contrast, there are those who understand there is more to life than fame and money. For example, a young, talented Megan Boudreaux graduated from university and started a career in the health industry. She was ready to take on any challenge and soon found herself enroute to Haiti for work. As she prepared to leave Haiti, she met a little girl dressed in rags who appeared to be starving.

Boudreaux left but never forgot the little girl. In a short time, she quit her job, sold all she had, and moved to Haiti without a job or a plan or a place to live. She found the little girl she remembered, and discovering she was an orphan, adopted her. She then started a school for at-risk children. Today, she runs a thriving nonprofit called Respire Haiti – with a school for 500 children, a health clinic, a café, and a recycling center.

She could have made more money and collected more possessions had she kept her job in the U.S. but today she sleeps well in Haiti, content in the knowledge she's changing lives as she teaches families to know a God who loves and cares about each of them.

Read Matthew 25:34-36. Boudreaux has found the secret to the Kingdom living - what is it?

Day 2 – Focus

Yesterday we met Megan Boudreaux who found contentment, significance, and peace in her life in Christ. Last week, we learned about another woman who was seeking fulfillment. As the conversation between Jesus and the woman at the well began to wind down, He made a stunning revelation - offering her a piece of information He had not yet shared with anyone else.

Reread John 4: 25-26. What did He tell her?

____

____

____

She told Him she knew the Messiah was coming. He then proclaimed, "I am He, you don't have to wait any longer or look any further."

The Samaritan woman was the first person to whom Jesus revealed His true identity - and it was quite a surprise. There was no audience present, no news reporters on the scene, no social media influencers posting, no film crew recording - just a quiet conversation between Jesus and an outcast over a drink of water.

Jesus met her where she was, at her point of need, and revealed His true identity based on her need. He asked for a drink of water, but He gave her so much more in return—the truth of who He was, the forgiveness of her past, the promise of eternal life, and hope for the future. With that, the private conversation was over because she was so excited she ran to tell everyone in town. They listened, and many believed, and those who did begged Jesus to stay and tell them more.

Day 3 - Foundation

Jesus had an unexpected conversation with an unlikely woman looking for love in all the wrong places and it resulted in the first evangelist in the New Testament. She almost seemed to get who Jesus was and what He was on earth to do better than even His disciples did. It's a compelling contrast - while they were in town purchasing food (and not making any new converts, by the way), she was being fed by Jesus, and soon would be on her way to help transform her city with the good news of the Messiah.

Whenever Jesus came along with the messages of living water, the bread of life, and grace, most people sat up and listened. Are you listening to the One who can give you the bread of life and the living water you crave?

____

____

Are you ready to turn away from the hollow offerings of the world to something much, much better?

____

____

When you feel overwhelmed with hunger and thirst for things you know are not healthy or good for you, Jesus can satisfy those longings with living water. He loves you, cares for you, and longs to fill the emptiness of your soul. Through Him, you have the ultimate victory over sins holding you down and keeping you from moving forward. He promises no more permanent emptiness, no more unquenchable longing for satisfaction. God offers you love and grace, and He is enough.

Day 4 – Reflect

Think about a craving with which you've struggled. How have you gained victory over this craving or at least kept it under control?

____

____

If you haven't yet gained victory, have you consistently invited Jesus into the struggle?

____

____

Could your craving be related to something deeper?

____

____

Like the woman at the well, many of us are yearning for happiness and fulfillment but not looking in the right place.

How can you confront this craving today after taking a fresh look at Jesus' words to the Samaritan woman?

____

____

____

____

Day 5 – Journal – Affirmations

Write down a prayer to the Lord Jesus and ask Him to fill your thirst with His living water, using some of the words and ideas from the passage in John 4:1-42.

Conclusion: A Better You

You did it! You completed the study, read the Bible through using S.O.A.P., and are well on your way to being a better you! As we close out the study, write one final prayer, thanking God for guiding you along the journey of transformation, transparency, freedom, identity, and outrageous love!

____

____

____

____

____

____

____

____

____

____

____